The Power
To Love

AuthorHouse™
1663 Liberty Drive
Bloomington, IN 47403
www.authorhouse.com
Phone: 1-800-839-8640

First published by AuthorHouse   6/29/2010

ISBN: 978-1-4520-3760-8 (e)
ISBN: 978-1-4520-3759-2 (hc)
ISBN: 978-1-4520-3758-5 (sc)

Library of Congress Control Number: 2010908606

Printed in the United States of America
Bloomington, Indiana

This book is printed on acid-free paper.

Preface

As a young pastor of a small church, I knew that loving others was not only the "new commandment" Jesus left with his disciples, but was the crowning virtue of the Christian life. Although I knew it was important, I just didn't know how to do it. Neither did I know how to teach others how to do it. Like so many others, I made the mistake in thinking that because people were physically healthy, they could love others. In my simplistic, if not idealistic world, loving others was just a matter of choice. If you are healthy you simply chose to love them and it will happen, especially if you have such a marvelous example in the life of Jesus.

Over the years God has patiently revealed that loving others is not as simple as it may sound. He has taught me, both academically and experientially, that loving others requires supernatural empowerment. I have discovered how utterly useless it is to urge people to love one another based on their natural abilities and their choice alone. In fact, it can be dangerous in that it produces such personal frustration that it undermines what relational benefits may have existed. People simply cannot love others like Christ in their own strength no matter how hard they might try!

The "Power to Love" is a study of the things needed to actually love others like Christ. The old saying, "you cannot give what you do not have" is no where more true than when it comes to giving others the love of God. Divine love, God's love, is supernatural in the sense that it cannot be generated by the natural effort of us human beings. We need empowerment by God, Himself, to be able to share His love with others in our everyday relationships. What I have discovered over the years is that God is happy to give us that empowerment! He not only commands us to love one another, but with that command he delights in giving us the power to do so.

In the context of their ministry of loving others, Jesus promised his disciples that whatever they asked in His name, he would do it that the Father may be glorified (John 14:13). When we ask the Father to give us the love we need to relate to others we are guaranteed to receive it. Our relationships, then, may be based on the supernatural empowerment of God's love given freely to us rather than our natural affections that are inadequate and invariably end in strife and despair. In this study I hope to demonstrate that such relational empowerment is not only possible, but may be freely enjoyed by all who will ask for it. May God open the eyes of your heart to know the dimensions of his love for you that you might share it with others.

John C. Glenn
December, 2009

Acknowledgements

I want to thank the many people who have made this series possible through their prayers and dedication to living out the "critical event". A special thanks to Jim Groth for his work in preparing the manuscript and writing the companion workbook. I also want to thank Roger Garramore and the men seeking recovery at the Safe Harbor Life Center who implemented this series as part of the Journey to Freedom recovery program and sought to practice these principles in their own lives. Finally, I am grateful for the people who meet at the Church in the Woods every week to practice that critical event of loving one another like Christ.

Dedications

This book is dedicated to my wife, Sandi, who has been supernaturally empowered to live with me for the last 37 years. Her willingness to learn and live what it takes to relate not only to me, but to all those we serve, is a continuous source of strength.

Contents

1. Foundations:
The Critical Event

After thirty-plus years of counseling, I've noticed that people have a tough time relating well to each other. Regardless of the context (family, work, school, church, etc.) relationships are hard to build and easy to loose. Family relationships can be especially painful. The heartbreaking effect of divorce not only hurt the married couple struggling with their own frustrations, but also causes a great deal of pain for their children and their extended family members. The misery of job dissatisfaction can, in many cases, be traced back to relational difficulties between employees and their co-workers or boss. Often we find ourselves trying to cope with an obnoxious neighbor or even embroiled in a nasty church split. These and similar problems have, at their core, the personal inability to relate to others in a healthy way.

This is true even among those people who are religious, including those who are called Christians. That's because religious people spend most all their energy trying to appease God by what they do and don't do and are too self-absorbed to really care about others. In fact, some of the meanest people I've known have been self-righteous Christians who are frustrated with themselves and others. They are either too busy judging and criticizing others or trying too hard to gain their approval to really love them. Like the original disciples of Jesus, we often find ourselves asking, "Which one of us is the greatest in the kingdom?" rather than "How can I love the people around me?"

What is desperately needed in today's world is what I call the "critical event"...loving one another just like Jesus loves us. I call it the "critical" event because no matter what else must be done in the context of the home, the job, the church, or the community loving others is absolutely critical to healthy relationships and a satisfying life. When married couples learn to love each other in the same way Jesus loves them they can endure the natural periods of disenchantment when the romance wears off their marriage. When parents learn to practice this critical event with their kids we will have a new generation of well adjusted and powerful youth entering our society. As workers are motivated with the love of God in the workplace, there is not only a dramatic change in production and efficiency, but also a new level of creativity and innovation. When community groups celebrate and practice the "critical event" we can experience a true culture of life.

But what is needed to actually practice this "critical event? Obviously, it doesn't just happen naturally. The power to love others in the same way God loves us is what true Christianity is all about. While faith may be viewed as the very foundation of true Christianity, love is the final product. Our faith in the gospel of God's grace works itself out in our everyday lives as genuine love for others. So much so that James insists that our faith is demonstrated by our acts of compassion without which it is "dead" (James 2). The power to love others like Christ is what I call relational empowerment. It's not a result of our own efforts or choice alone, but comes from the quality of our relationship with God.

Biblical Christianity is not so much a religion, as it is a two-fold love relationship…a vertical relationship between you and God, and a horizontal relationship between you and others. In addition, the quality of our relationship to others is directly determined by our relationship to God. In a very real sense you could say that our relationship to others reflects the quality of our relationship to God. The ability to love others in the same way God loves us is determined by our willingness to receive God's love ourselves.

In today's secular culture many sincere, but misguided people are trying to develop a loving relationship with others apart from a relationship to God. Recognizing the need for loving relationships is not enough, we must also have the power to develop and maintain them. Unfortunately, being able to build and maintain healthy and satisfying relationships in the home or community does not just happen automatically. As a matter of fact, our natural disposition as human beings coupled with the conditioning of our society often makes our relationships to others a very troublesome if not painful experience. Much of our suffering on a personal level is the direct result of the difficulties we encounter when trying to build or maintain relationships.

In this study we want to recognize and receive the power to love others like Christ. Our method will be to focus on the personal, communication, and relational skills needed to empower us to practice the critical event in every aspect of our lives. Since both the power to love and the love itself originates with God, we begin with our relationship to him.

Turning the Relational Corner

The primary relationship we must consider is that vertical relationship between them and God. It's primary because apart from our relationship to God we cannot hope to have a healthy relationship with others. This is illustrated throughout the Bible, but clearly stated in John's first general letter (1John 4: 7, 8). The apostle writes, *"Beloved, let us love one another: for love is of God; and every one that loveth is born of God, and knoweth God. He that loveth not knoweth not God; for God is love."*

The best biblical term for relational empowerment may simply be "love". The most healthy and satisfying relationships we can experience with others is summarized by the biblical phrase, "love one another". Not only did Jesus leave us with the "new" command to love one another (John 13:34,35), but the same idea is presented over and over throughout the writings of the New Testament. It is for this reason that I refer to loving others as the "critical event". No matter what else we may do in the course of our daily lives, what God is concerned with the most is that we love others the way he does. Note that this takes supernatural empowerment since Jesus qualified the manner in which we are to love others by the phrase "as I have loved you". This means that the love we are to give others is the same love that we receive from Jesus, himself. It is this supernatural quality of his love that makes the commandment "new".

It is that kind of love that John calls us to when he calls us to love one another and explains that "love is of God". Notice first how he addresses us... he calls us "beloved". This implies that we are the ones God loves, and the ones who have received his love. To the extent that we receive the love of God as the "beloved" we are able to give that love to others. It is impossible to give what we do not have. We cannot love others unless we have received that love ourselves. This is especially true since the love we are talking about is not what we are naturally capable of producing in and of ourselves, but rather what God works in us. This is why the vertical relationship is the primary relationship.

"For love is of God" is the way John tells us that all love originates with God. The source of the love we are to share with others is not found in anyone or anything other than God himself. It cannot be mustered up from within ourselves, but must be received from God as the never ending source. In a later study we will consider the exact nature of that love, but for now we simply need to recognize that it is received only through our vertical relationship with God. The relational empowerment we are seeking to understand is simply the ability to receive and give the love that comes only from God.

John goes on to describe that relational empowerment by revealing the two conditions that must be met in order to love others. "*And every one that loveth is born of God and knoweth God*". The first requirement for being able to love others like God is to be born of God. By this he simply means the miraculous way that God transforms us from the natural self-centered and dysfunctional persons we were born as to the new persons he has made us to be in Christ. This is the same birth that Jesus told the Jewish teacher, Nicodemus, about during that evening interview recorded in John's gospel. It is the very heart issue of the gospel of grace that declares that God, through his Spirit puts to death the old person we were, and raises up a new person in Christ. This change in identity is what allows us to receive the love of God as we become "partakers of the divine nature" which is love. Because we are born of God we are capable of loving others like him.

But have you ever known someone besides yourself that has been born of God and continues to be selfish and unloving? Of course you have. Some of the meanest people I have ever known have been born again Christians. How can this be? How can those who have received the love of God not love others like God? John goes on to answer this in the statement that follows. The second requirement for being empowered to love others is simply described as "*knoweth God*". By this he means that all who are going to love others like God must not only be born of Him (giving them the potential to love), but also must have an intimate, personal knowledge of God as well.

Knowing God does not mean that we simply know about Him...it implies that we have a very intimate and personal relationship with God. The best way to conceive of this is to describe that intimate relationship with God in terms of our personal needs. To know God intimately is to experience the ways he satisfies our deepest needs and to realize how we satisfy him as well. Because of his love for us God continually satisfies our needs for security and significance on a personal level as well as our physical needs. He not only meets our needs for unconditional love, acceptance and forgiveness, but he also gives us a sense of importance, purpose and adequacy. We, in turn are capable of satisfying his needs through the faith we express in loving him as well as his own people.

John assures us that those who don't love don't know God on this intimate and personal level. While they may be born of God, they are still "babes" in Christ and have not yet matured enough to care about, much less love others. Obviously, then, relational empowerment stems from the intimate and experiential knowledge of God who is love.

The personal transformation of being born of God gives us the potential to love others and the intimate knowledge of God allows us to actually express His love in our relationships. Our faith in our new identity in Christ satisfies our deepest needs for love and respect. This faith produces genuine hope (a joyful and confident expectation about our own future) that frees us to actually think about someone besides ourselves regardless of the circumstances or situations we experience. The expression of love for others generates the various ways and means of relational ministry. All of this is what we mean by the term, relational empowerment, or the power to love.

Relational Empowerment Goals

The ultimate goal of relational empowerment may be summarized in terms of the spiritual maturity called for in the Scriptures. Jesus told his worried and self-centered disciples that when they loved one another like he loved them that all men would know they were his disciples. It is not our religious behavior or activities that signify our true spiritual condition, but rather our ability to practice the critical event under the worst of conditions. True faith in the message Jesus gave us will always lead us to the personal transformation needed to be free from our natural selfishness long enough to actually love others.

Paul referred to our ability to love others with the love of Christ as a sure sign of spiritual maturity. To the Corinthians he complained that he was not able to speak to them as those who were spiritually mature, but as babes...specifically mentioning the envying, strife, and divisions due to a lack of love (1 Corinthians 3:1-3). There he also noted that he was unable to feed them the "meat" of the word. Due to their lack of maturity, they could only receive the "milk" of the word. By this he meant that the Corinthians needed to focus on all that God had done for them in Christ (i.e. the milk of the word); and were not yet able to hear what God intended to do through them for others (i.e. the meat of the word). Later in the same letter he contrasts the "more excellent way" of loving others with the typical religious game playing of "coveting the best gifts" and expounds on the power and virtues of real love (1 Corinthians 13).

Likewise, to the Galatians Paul wrote that the only thing that really counts with God is our faith continually working itself out in love for others (Galatians 5:6). Contrary to modern religious thought, it's not what we do or do not do that impresses God, but rather our ability to trust his provisions for us so that we might be free to love others. Our faith in the gospel of grace creates a hope in us about our own situation so that we are liberated to think about and care for others. This kind of love, Paul says, actually fulfills the righteous demands of God's law (Galatians 5:14).

The goal of relational empowerment is ultimately concerned with equipping us, as believers, to serve others. We call this relational ministry, or simply loving others like Christ, and recognize that the quality of our relationships is determined by our ability to love in this way. Whether it is in the home, on the job, or in the community our ability to relate to others around us is foundational to healthy living. Those who are empowered to do so not only experience the satisfaction of a meaningful life themselves, but also enlighten and encourage others to healthy living.

Relational Empowerment Strategies

As we have noted, loving others like Christ is not automatic in our natural condition. All humans are born with self-centeredness and cannot automatically think about, much less, love one another. In addition, all of us have been disappointed, hurt, or even abused by others at some time. The most common and natural response to such offenses is an attitude of resentment and bitterness. We seek to insulate ourselves from further pain by developing coping strategies motivated by hatred rather than love. The combination of our own natural selfishness and the coping strategies based on hatred must be considered before we can truly practice the critical event.

Before trying to reach out to and love others it is necessary to consider our own condition. This is what Jesus referred to as removing the "beam" from our own eye before we try to remove the "splinter" from our brother's eye. In his Sermon on the Mount, Jesus warns against trying to love someone else (take the splinter out of their eye) without dealing with our own issues (getting the telephone pole out of our own eye). Unless we are willing to let God change our selfish nature we cannot really love or help anyone else. The first strategy, then, is to allow God to change us from the inside out. He must transform us from a self-centered "taker" to a loving "giver". Loving others like Christ always begins with receiving his love for us. Over the years I have witnessed people trying to love others without being changed by Gods love. It always ends in failure. At best they present a religious façade of tolerance and acceptance, but soon they retreat from the relationship with a multitude of excuses and rationalizations.

In a similar way Paul warns that before we try to restore one "overtaken in a fault" we should consider our self lest we also be tempted. In Galatians 6:1 he commands us to restore (not simply condemn) one who is overtaken in a fault or literally, "caught in a trespass". These people are behaving badly and deserve to be punished in some way. But Paul calls on us to restore them! Then he adds the phrase, "considering yourself lest you also be tempted". By this he means there is some work to do on ourselves if we are going to restore rather than condemn those who act out. This work will have to do with our own fleshly attitude of hatred and bitterness toward them. Not only do we need a strategy of God's love changing us from the inside out, but we also need a strategy of forgiveness.

In his discussion of forgiveness in Matthew 18, Jesus referred to this strategy in graphic language as "cutting off your own hand or foot or poking out your own eye". This implies that allowing God to remove the hatred from our heart is going to involve some self-inflicted pain as we recall the conflict and hurt and ask God to forgive us for hating those who hurt us. The natural reaction of the flesh to any kind of disappointment or hurt is hatred. While we generally do not want to admit our hate in the flesh, it is there none the less. Only when we are willing to identify our own hatred toward those who have been overtaken in a fault and hurt us will we allow God to forgive (or send away) that hatred. Our freedom to love others like Christ can only be obtained by our willingness to be forgiven. Much more will be said about this process in later studies, but for now it is sufficient to recognize forgiveness as a two way street. Like divine love, we cannot give what we do not have. We must receive forgiveness before we can give it to others.

Relational Empowerment Skills

Relational empowerment involves learning and practicing three sets of skills (personal skills, communication skills, and relational skills) on a daily basis. The first set is referred to as personal skills since they are primarily concerned with our own personal preparation to relate to other in a healthy way. They include the following:

Personal Skills
- Cognitive restructuring
  - o   Changing beliefs about ourselves
- Emotional management
  - o   Controlling our own emotions
- Behavioral redirection
  - o   Motivational change from manipulation to ministry
- Spiritual enlightenment
  - o   Developing authentic vs. toxic faith

As will be discussed in the next chapter these skills are essential to develop the hope we need to endure the inevitable conflict and tension of day to day relationships. Attempting to love others like Christ without these personal skills will likely lead to religious and superficial performance at best, and intensified conflicts at worst. Being willing to challenge our own beliefs about our worth as persons, assume responsibility for managing our own emotions, checking our own motivation in all situations, and seeking spiritual guidance through authentic faith will equip us to interact with others in a constructive way. These personal skills allow us to take a "personal inventory" concerning our behavior, emotions, and beliefs on a daily basis. The importance of such is the honest recognition of our own weakness and need for divine empowerment in our relationships.

The communication skills necessary for relational empowerment include a basic understanding of the communication cycle, active listening, speaking the truth in love, and differentiating core issues from superficial issues.

Communication Skills
- The Communication Cycle
- Active Listening
- Speaking the truth in love
- Addressing core issues

Since the tower of Babel when God "confounded their language" (Genesis 11: 7) the human race has suffered from a terrible lack of these skills. Just because we are talking with one another there is no guarantee that we are actually communicating. Often we say more through our silence, facial expressions, tone of voice, or posture and than we do with our words and the quality of our relationships suffers because of it. In addition to the male and female differences in communication there are many other obstacles that only the supernatural power of the Spirit can overcome.

Developing and utilizing communication skills depends first on our communication with God and then others. Because we are spiritual as well as physical and personal beings, we actually have the ability to communicate with God. Unfortunately, most people have trouble "hearing" God and are generally confused about their prayer life. It is vital that we learn to recognize God's voice so that we may be skilled in communicating with others.

The final set of skills needed for relational empowerment is called relational skills. They are really just expressions of divine love as follows:

Relational Skills
- Warn the unruly
  - Confronting inappropriate behavior
- Comfort the hurting
  - Consoling the emotionally distraught
- Support the weak in the faith
  - Counsel those who believe they are worthless

These relational skills will likely be applied within the same relationship. That is, you may confront someone who is behaving inappropriately and then comfort him as he seeks help and support him in his efforts to apply the gospel to his situation. Although these relational skills may be utilized individually according to the needs of others, their most common use will be in the context of a single more intimate relationship. It is doubtful that you will be called upon to confront the inappropriate behavior of a stranger or some-one you are just barely acquainted with. Usually we must have a more intimate relationship in which we have, "earned the right" to confront, warn, or support.

Building on the other two sets of skills, the relational skills are true expressions of divine love rather than humanistic or romantic love. Note the difference in the following contrasts:

God's Love		Human Love
• Unconditional	vs.	Conditional
• Sacrificial	vs.	Convenient
• Initiating	vs.	Passive
• Eternal	vs.	Temporary
• Intelligent	vs.	Romantic

The relational skills we are seeking to develop are those that allow us to love others in the same manner as God. Because such love is intelligent as well as unconditional, sacrificial, eternal and initiating, it always seeks what is best for the one loved rather than simply what will make them feel better. Relational empowerment, then, can be described as the God-given ability to confront others without condemning them, comfort others without enabling them, and support them without any strings attached.

Summary

Relational empowerment is simply the supernatural ability God gives us to love others in the same way he does. Having received the love of God for ourselves, we are free to share that love with others as he gives us opportunity to practice the critical event at home with our families as well as at work or in the community.

The developmental analogy used in the scriptures describes relational empowerment as a sure sign of spiritual maturity. The "babe" in Christ requires the "milk of the word" (all that the Bible declares God has done for us), whereas the mature or adult child of God is able to eat the "meat of the word" (all that the Bible declares that God will do through us for others). Being empowered by God to care for and love others is a sure sign of maturity. It was this ability to love others that Jesus identified as the badge of true discipleship promising that by this shall all men know that you are my disciples.

2. Cognitive Restructuring

Personal Skills Needed for Our Relationship to God

Loving others like Christ is not natural to human beings. Being born selfish and self-centered, we naturally can't think of anyone else, much less love them with God's love. This is why we all need relational *empowerment*. We must receive the transforming grace of God to be able to actually care about others; that empowerment is what we are seeking in this study. So before we try to understand what we should say or how we should behave when loving others, we need to consider what is necessary to break our own selfish thinking and actions. This is what I call the personal skills.

Generally, the personal skills needed to express the love of Christ to others may be viewed as receiving God's love for us. As stated earlier, we cannot give what we do not have. If we are going to express the love of God as we are encouraged to do, we must be skilled in receiving it. Unfortunately, many Christians struggle on this very first point. They may understand that God is supposed to love them, or even that he has loved them both intellectually and theologically; but they are not at all convinced that he really does love them personally. To put it in terms we have already used, they are struggling with their vertical relationship with God. How do we know that? Just look at their horizontal relationships with their family, boss, friends, or others.

> They may understand that God is supposed to love them, or even that he has loved them both intellectually and theologically; but they are not at all convinced that he really does love them personally.

25

The apostle John makes it very clear that the quality of our relationship with God is mirrored in our relationships with others. If we have trouble getting along with the people around us, we need to carefully consider our own relationship with God. This is especially true when we consider the command of Jesus to "love" our enemies.

The first place to begin in any relationship is to consider our relationship to God; not just academically or theologically, but personally. It is in the strength of our personal relationship to God that we find the empowerment needed to relate to others. As Jesus said he could do nothing apart from the Father, so we can do nothing apart from him…including the ability to love others the way he does.

The specific personal skills needed in our personal relationship with God are as follows:

1. Cognitive restructuring - changing our thinking about ourselves
2. Emotional management - controlling our own feelings
3. Behavioral redirection - changing our motives from manipulation to ministry
4. Spiritual enlightenment - listening to the inner voice of God

Without these personal skills we are not in any position to relate to others in a healthy way. Such unskilled relationships always end in disaster and cause enormous pain to all concerned. Broken relationships in the family may plague us with grief and sorrow for years. Friendships go sour and business deals fall apart due to unskilled relationships. The inability to practice these relational skills prevents us from receiving God's love and power we need to care about and love others, and we easily fall prey to the vicious cycles of the dysfunctional world in which we live.

Repentance: 180 Degree Change in Thinking

In this chapter we will consider the first of these skills we simply call "cognitive restructuring". The term, "cognitive" has to do with our thinking while "restructuring" simply implies a change. Taken together this simply means a change in our thinking. Before we can change our behavior (both verbal and non verbal) toward others, it is necessary to change the feelings that underlie that behavior. In order to change our feelings we must change our thinking. So the first skill we will consider is that of cognitive restructuring or simply changing our thinking.

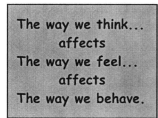

The way we think... affects
The way we feel... affects
The way we behave.

The best biblical description of cognitive restructuring may be the simple word, "repent". Literally in the Greek language of the New Testament this word is translated from a compound word "meta" meaning change and "nous" meaning mind. The combination literally means a 180 degree change in thinking. So when the Bible calls on us to repent it really is calling for a 180 degree change in our thinking.

Repentance means changing your mind or your thinking. Our present word of metamorphosis expresses this well. It is not so much feeling sorry for your misdeeds, or even trying harder in the future but a call to look at the world and yourself and God in a brand new way. It is not so much a turning away from a sinful lifestyle as it is a challenge to examine your core ideas about how to please God and how to attain his blessings. Of course since sin is defined as unbelief then that alone changes the traditional view of repentance. In this respect, repentance means changing your mind about Christ and turning to him. Repentance is not so much about what we do but why we do it. It is about the core beliefs which motivate our day to day activities and our point of view. It is a metamorphosis at the core level of our being

In repentance we view ourselves in a whole new way. We see ourselves as saints by God's grace and not as sinners. This is the way God sees us and our minds should align with his. This is a radical change in thinking and a brand new viewpoint about ourselves and our relationship with God.

Repentance is a 180 degree turn in heart, mind, trust, and understanding which will eventually lead to a better life style. This change involves our thinking, the way we read scripture, the way we treat others, our relationship to God and provides the motivation of faith, hope and love, rather than fear, guilt and pride.

In summary repentance is not so much a turning from sin (a byproduct) but from the conditioning of the world which is crafted to take our eyes and dependence off of Jesus and on to ourselves and others. Cognitive restructuring requires we restructure our perception of reality and of things of importance. It involves repentance but it goes deeper in that it requires more than a superficial change.

Changing Core Beliefs about Ourselves

But what are we to change about our thinking? To keep it personal and relevant we need to understand that this skill demands we learn to change our thinking about ourselves. Naturally, we are born with an innate sense of worthlessness that drives us to do and say things to make ourselves look or feel good. That selfishness, as we have already noted, is at the root of all our relational difficulties.

> Rather than view ourselves as being somehow worthless, we need to be able to think of ourselves as being worthwhile or worthy.

The change in thinking called for in cognitive restructuring, first and foremost, concerns our thinking about ourselves. Rather than view ourselves as being somehow worthless, we need to be able to think of ourselves as being worthwhile or worthy. Until this change occurs we cannot hope to feel worthy, act worthy, or relate to others well. In short, unless we can change the way we naturally think about ourselves we will continue to relate to others as "takers" rather than "givers" and our relationships will suffer.

To help us understand this personal skill of cognitive restructuring we must identify the basic assumptions or beliefs we have about ourselves. Because we are personal beings we have a set of personal as well as physical needs that must be met each day. Just as surely as we need air to breathe each day, we need a sense of worth as a person. Each day we need to know that we are secure and significant as a person. That is, we need to know and believe that we are loved unconditionally; accepted just as we are, and forgiven for our defects.

Likewise we need to know that we are significant as persons; that we are important, that we have meaning and purpose in our lives, and that we are adequate or able to fulfill that purpose. Just as we may experience physical hunger and thirst each day, our soul or person hungers for love and thirsts for respect. These personal needs have to be met for us to live and relate in a healthy way.

Specifically, our basic assumptions about ourselves and what it takes to make us worthy, based upon those assumptions, must be identified and corrected. According to the Bible God has already done all that is necessary in Christ to make us secure and significant as persons. Because of our union with Christ we share in his worth so that we are just a secure and significant as he is. This truth is illustrated all the way through the Scriptures, but is stated clearly in Paul's letters in Romans 6-7 and Ephesians 1. God has made us new creations in Christ, perfect in his sight; we are eternally secure in His love and significant in His plan. This is why we call it the gospel or the "good news. Unfortunately, we have a tendency to lose sight of this good news and fall back into the natural mind set that we are some how less worthy (i.e. less secure or less significant). This is especially the case when we focus our attention on our current situation in this world of ours or evaluate ourselves according to the opinion of others or our own performance.

Because we have been conditioned our whole life to base our worth on anything and everything except God and what he has done for us in Christ, we often find ourselves thinking that we are not loved, accepted or forgiven; or that we are not important, have no purpose, or adequacy. This kind of thinking is reinforced in our thinking by our awareness of our own failures, the negative comments and opinions of others and difficult circumstances in which we might find ourselves.

Each day we have a choice as to what we are going to believe about ourselves. We can either chose to believe that we are worthy or chose to believe that we are somehow worthless. That choice is ours. Despite the fact that the circumstances and evidence around us may seem to be so overwhelming, we still have a choice. No matter how you have failed, no matter what others think or say about you, and no matter how terrible your circumstances may be; you have a choice to believe you are worthless or worthy. It is this choice that is at the heart of cognitive restructuring.

At this point it may be useful to phrase this choice in more familiar, if some what artificial language. When we try to identify the thinking that must be changed it helps to put it in terms of changing false assumptions to true assumptions. The format used to describe a false assumption is simply, "I will be worthy if..." This statement needs to be seen as false regardless of what we might use to complete it. When we say, "I **_will be_** worthy if... what we are really saying is "right now I am worthless, but I will be worthy if..." The statement that we are right now worthless is what makes this a false assumption. God says he has made us to be worthy by what he has already done for us in Christ, therefore, any statement to the contrary is false.

Replacing Lies with Truth

Cognitive restructuring involves a 180 degree change in our thinking from the false to the true assumptions. Rather than believing "I will be worthy if..." we chose to believe "I am worthy because of who God has made me to be. This choice will usually not seem to be so clear in most situations, neither will it feel right since we are likely to have a set of troubling circumstances or negative opinions of others, or a sense of failure associated with it. However, based on the word of God alone we must learn to make this choice for truth in spite of the opposition we might encounter.

To help us identify some of the more common false assumptions about our worth we draw from the work of Robert McGee, the author of *The Search for Significance*. In his book he list four "lies" about our worth as persons that are common to all. We may view these as categories of false assumptions that typically plague us daily. The first he calls the "performance trap". The basic lie here may be stated as, "I will be worthy if I meet up to certain standards". Closely associated with that lie is what he calls the "blame game"... "People who fail are unworthy of love and deserve to be punished" or "I will be worthy if I can find fault or blame someone else". The third lie is "I will be worthy if I get the approval of certain other people" or what he simply calls an "approval addiction". The last category he refers to as simply "shame" and is a resignation to the fact that "I am what I am, I'm hopeless and I will never change". If we think of McGee's lies as categories of false assumptions we can easily see how there could be an infinite number of these in our minds daily. The skill of cognitive restructuring is the skill to challenge and change these lies into the truth.

McGee goes on to contrast the false assumptions we have just outlined with the Biblical truth. Citing the biblical concepts of regeneration, justification, propitiation and reconciliation he systematically counters each of the lies with the biblical truth of our worth in Christ. Our purpose here is not to review the details of his work in countering the lies, but to demonstrate that true repentance involves choosing to believe biblical truth rather than lies about our worth. Magee's conclusion is best expressed in the affirmation, "Because of Christ's redemption I am an awesome spirit being of magnificent worth as a person..."

In Romans 6-8 Paul tells us "the good news for believers", that we are dead to sin, dead to the law, and alive in Christ. Likewise in Ephesians 1 he writes that we are blessed with all spiritual blessings and goes on to list them out. Clearly, the message of the Bible is that we are truly loved of God and important in his eternal plan. Cognitive restructuring is simply changing our thinking from the natural, "I will be worthy if..." to the supernatural, "I am worthy because of Christ". Such a change in our thinking is what repentance is really about.

True repentance, however, cannot be separated from the exercise of faith. Even when believing a lie about your worth, you are still exercising faith. The false assumptions of our worth are beliefs we hold to firmly because they involve our personal needs. We cannot simply quit believing in and depending on lies, we must have something else to hang on to before we are willing to let go of those lies. We will never let go of our false assumptions unless we are able to firmly lay hold of the true ones. We do this by reviewing over and over again the glorious gospel of grace that tells us all that God has done for us in Christ that we could not do for ourselves. We cannot believe or depend on something we have never heard. We must rehearse again and again the fact that God has crucified the selfish person we were and raised us up to be a brand new person in Christ. We need to focus on our new identity in Christ as being holy and with out blame before him in love. As we "look into the mirror" of God's word and steadfastly behold the "glory of the Lord" (who we are in Christ) we are changed into the same image by his indwelling Spirit (2 Corinthians 3:18). As will be discussed in a later chapter, it is his Spirit that actually renews our minds and allows us to develop the skill of cognitive restructuring. For now it is sufficient to realize that this personal skill is the way we receive the love of God we must share with others.

Summary

In many respects the personal skill of cognitive restructuring is the most foundational of all the skills we will consider. Without the daily "repentance and faith" described here we can never hope to manage our emotions, redirect our behavior, walk in the power of the Spirit, communicate effectively with God or others, much less love others like Christ. We can compare this personal skill to that of breathing on a physical level. Although we have additional physical needs, the need to breathe is perhaps the most foundational. We can go days without water and weeks or even months without food, but we can only survive minutes without air. Likewise, we cannot breathe enough air today to last us tomorrow. Breathing is essential because the need for air is continuous. So also is repentance and faith in the personal realm. On a minute by minute, day by day basis we need to know that we are truly secure and significant as persons. The ability to challenge our false assumptions and replace them with biblical assumptions of our worth as a person is analogous to our soul "breathing" the pure "air" of the gospel of grace as opposed to the "polluted air" of the natural false assumptions about our worth.

Just as surely as we continuously breathe to maintain our physical lives we must also continuously trust in something or someone to meet our need for worth. At a preconscious level (just below the surface of our awareness) we are talking to ourselves about what we think we need to make ourselves secure or significant as persons all the time. The "polluted" self talk our soul naturally breathes is the false assumption we have identified in the, "I will be worthy if..." format. Cognitive restructuring involves replacing these false assumptions with the Biblical assumptions in the "I am worthy because…" format. This skill allows the soul to breathe the pure air of the gospel of grace and prepares it to develop all the other skills needed to love others like Christ.

Exercises

1. Identifying our own false assumptions is the first step in the personal skill of cognitive restructuring. Write, "I will be worthy if…" at the top of a sheet of paper, and then list seven (7) false assumptions that come to your mind. Ask God to reveal these beliefs to you.

2. Review specific times or situations in which you became personally upset in order to begin to recognize false assumptions. Because we do not get upset about things that do not affect us personally, any situation that produces strong emotions gives us a place to look for the false assumptions that produce those feelings. Briefly describe the situation and the emotions associated with one of the false assumptions you have identified.)

3. Turn your worksheet over and write at the top of the page, "I am worthy because…" For every false assumption listed on the front side of the page find a biblical assumption (Bible verse or verses) that state you are worthy (secure or significant) as a person. These seven biblical assumptions of worth constitute the "pure air" your soul needs to breathe each day.

4. Cognitive restructuring requires us to counter the lies of our own false assumptions with the truth of the biblical assumptions of our worth. To become skilled at doing this we need to practice not only identifying the false, but also believing the true assumptions as a conscious choice made each day. Whenever you begin to feel bad or discouraged, you may be assured it is because you are naturally believing

34

the lies about your self rather than the truth of God's Word. It is at that time you need to identify the false and choose to believe the true assumptions.

3. Emotional Management

Empowered to Love

The most difficult obstacle to overcome in relating well with others is that of our own emotions. It is exceptionally difficult, if not totally impossible, to love other people when we ourselves are hurting. When Jesus told his disciples he wanted them to love one another as he loved them, they were in no emotional condition to hear what he had to say. He had just revealed to them that he was leaving them and that they could not go with him any further. This

> It is exceptionally difficult, if not totally impossible, to love other people when we ourselves are hurting.

gave them all a "spiritual heart attack" because they were counting on him not only staying around, but also setting up a kingdom in which they could shine. Their false assumptions may have been something like, "I will be worthy if I can be recognized as the greatest" or "I will be worthy if I can be rich and famous in the kingdom". With such thinking the last thing on their minds was to love each other. So when Jesus announced his soon departure and commanded them to love each other it is doubtful that they were able to even accept it much less live it out.

We are much the same. As long as we are feeling ok, we may consider being nice to someone or even trying to love them. But when we are frustrated in one way or another we often find ourselves being short with our "loved ones" or even being downright mean. This is why the second personal skill, emotional management, is so vital to relational empowerment. In order to actually be able to love others like Christ we have to be able to control our feelings rather than be controlled by them. Like cognitive restructuring this skill is not something we do occasionally, but something we need to practice daily. It is essential to handle our own feeling appropriately to be able to care about much less love others. Because life has many trials and personal suffering associated with it, this skill is needed daily.

The Key to Emotional Management

The key to emotional management grows out of what we learned from cognitive restructuring. In order to understand this we need to consider where our emotions come from in the first place. Contrary to popular opinion, emotions do not simply fall out of the sky and neither are they produced solely by the things that happen to us. All of us have been conditioned to believe that we should feel bad when bad things happen to us. We believe it is the proper response to the unpleasant situation. For instance, if some one talks bad about me I might say that so and so hurt my feelings by what they said. The truth, however, is that it's not just what happens to me that determines how I feel, but also what I tell myself about my self in light of what happened that determines how I really feel. Psychologist Albert Ellis proposed what he called the ABC theory of emotions to

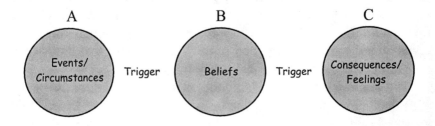

help us understand our own responsibility. He stated that the event (A) does not produce the consequence (C) by itself. In between A and C is B which stands for beliefs. According to his theory, what we believe about ourselves because of event A is the real determinant of our feelings. Although this puts a responsibility on us for our own emotions (we can't blame others or circumstances anymore); if we are willing to take this responsibility we find a key to emotional management.

Ellis makes sense. We have the ability to control what we feel in any situation by what we chose to believe about ourselves. Emotional management is possible if we understand the important role our self-talk plays in determining how we feel in any given situation. What we tell ourselves about ourselves when bad things happen to us is really what determines the quality of our feelings. Telling ourselves lies about our worth as persons, when bad things happen to us, turns our anger into hate, our hurt into self-pity, and our concern into worry. Telling ourselves the truth about our worth when bad things happen allows us to feel the negative emotions without letting them degenerate into sinful, destructive emotions.

Controlling our emotions, however, does not mean that we are able to avoid pain! It means that instead of falling into the destructive and sinful emotions when faced with a threatening situation we are able to endure the negative feelings without losing control. Rather than allowing our selves to slip into hatred, for instance, we are able to maintain a degree of divine love for those who make us angry. Instead of simply feeling sorry for ourselves when we are hurt, we are able to endure real agony with the "joy unspeakable and full of glory" that comes from genuine hope. Likewise, instead of becoming anxious we can actually face our fears with the "peace that passes all understanding".

As we will learn later, it is the role of the Comforter (the indwelling Holy Spirit) to provide us with the love, joy, and peace we need to prevent our negative feelings from degenerating into sinful, destructive emotions. Our part in that process, as always, is to simply believe the truth of the gospel regardless of how threatening the situation may appear. The good news about believers is that they really are secure in God's love and significant in God's plan no matter what their situation. It is our faith in this gospel that allows us to manage our own emotions despite the terrible circumstances of our lives. It is for this reason that we are encouraged to "count it all joy" when we face bad times and "rejoice in tribulation" believing that the trials we face will ultimately be worked out for good.

What Do We Believe

Since our beliefs determine the quality of our emotions it is important to consider just exactly what we must believe to manage our own emotions. Most of us have been conditioned with an "old covenant" mind set when it comes to suffering and hurt feelings. Frequently we make a "deal" with God that says something like, "I will try as hard as I can to be a good Christian and not screw up and God will not let anything bad happen to me or the people I love." The example of Jesus, himself, not withstanding, we still believe that we can avoid suffering and pain by what we do or do not do to please God. Although no one has ever been more obedient and suffered so much as Jesus, we somehow believe we can avoid bad things happening to us by trying hard to be good.

> We still believe that we can avoid suffering and pain by what we do or do not do to please God.

To help us come to a better understanding of suffering in general, and what we are to believe about ourselves in particular, we can apply an "eternal view of suffering".

Eternal View of Suffering

Do not be surprised (1 Peter 4:12)

– *Because we live in a sin-cursed world in sin-cursed bodies that are falling apart we all must suffer at some time. Peter warns us not to think of it as though some strange thing has happened to us when we suffer.*

— *Likewise, Paul tells us that it is given to us not only to believe on Jesus, but to also suffer for his sake. Because God has left us in this world and in these bodies to be Christ to others, we will have to suffer, but should not be surprised by it or take it as a sign of personal failure.*

See the end at the beginning (Romans 5:3-5)

— *Promises of positive outcomes to all forms of suffering are a great source of hope that allows us to persevere no matter what the trial. The ultimate end of all our suffering is the increased awareness of God's love, joy and peace.*
— *The "eternal" perspective allows us to believe there will be a positive outcome at the beginning of the trial. It is when we believe in this outcome even though it looks threatening and bad at the beginning that we demonstrate our faith.*

Know you cannot lose (Romans 8:28)

— *God assures us of victory... no matter what we must suffer, we will not lose in the end. We are told that "all things" (even our suffering) work together for our good.*
— *Despite all evidence to the contrary, we are not victims, but victors. In fact, we are called, "more than conquerors" even when it looks like we are going to lose.*

To the extent that we are willing to believe the biblical truth about ourselves in the middle of our suffering we are able to actually manage our own emotions. As mentioned earlier, this does not mean that we will not feel anger, anguish, or fear in our lives, but that we will not let those negative emotions control us as they degenerate into hatred, self-pity, and anxiety. In spite of feeling bad we are still able to act responsibly because we believe the gospel. This is emotional management. Telling ourselves the truth in the midst of our own suffering we are able to care about others regardless of our circumstances.

No one demonstrated emotional management better than Jesus. Being a "man of sorrows, acquainted with grief" he experienced all the negative emotions we will ever know. In the temple facing the religious leaders out to kill him, he felt real anger. In the garden he experience agonizing grief and astonishment. Being betrayed and arrested he felt the objective fear of impending death. Yet Jesus managed those intense negative emotions without ever once slipping into hatred, self-pity, or anxiety. In his greatest hour of suffering he was able to fulfill his responsibility of loving others and glorify the Father. Emotional management does not mean that we protect ourselves from hurt feelings, but that we learn how to deal with them in a healthy way.

What to do with Hurt Feelings

The natural way we lean to handle our hurt feeling is to either "stuff" them or "dump" them. We stuff our feelings when we deny that we have them or simply cover them up. This can be useful at first, but it will cause a lot of problems for us later. We might go on with our lives despite our hurt feelings, but unexpressed emotions can build up to the point where they can cause us to suffer physically from psychosomatic illnesses. Likewise, dumping our emotions indiscriminately on any one who will listen to us may take a serious toll on us relationally as well. No one likes to be around people who are constantly whining about their hurt feelings. But what do we do with our hurt feelings if we can't stuff or dump them? An important means of emotional management is needed, not so much as a ritual to be performed to get relief, but as a guide to responsible behavior in managing our emotions.

An important means of emotional management is needed, not so much as a ritual to be performed to get relief, but as a guide to responsible behavior in managing our emotions.

42

First, we need to fully acknowledge our feelings to God. This keeps us from dumping them on others who are not likely to be willing or able to take what we are feeling, much less help us. Like Jesus in the garden, we need to honestly tell the Father just exactly what we are feeling in no uncertain terms. Remember, God not only knows how we are feeling, but is also big enough, strong enough and willing to deal with it.

Second, we need to allow Him to affirm our own worth as persons. Our hurt feelings are directly related to our personal needs for worth. We are feeling bad, not just because some bad thing has happened to us, but also because we have begun to believe that we are somehow worth less as a person. Whatever time we take in dumping on God, we need to allow him time to affirm us as his child. This he does through the Comforter who renews our minds and guides us into all truth.

Finally, we need to commit ourselves to serving others regardless of our own feelings. We are not just faking it with others, but committing ourselves to be used of God to minister to the needs of others in spite of the fact that we do not feel good ourselves. If we are tempted to wait until we feel good to love others, we will never get around to doing so. But if we will commit ourselves to serving others in love regardless of how we feel, we will be surprised by how our feelings are changed by the Spirit as we actually begin to love others.

Summary

Emotional management is a most vital skill for relational empowerment. It not only allows us to cope with our own emotions, but also begins to teach us what we will need to help others who are hurting. Later in our study we will address, more specifically, what we have to give those who are hurting emotionally; but for now it is important to note that the comfort we receive as we practice the skill of emotional management is the very same comfort we will share with others who are suffering.

The key to emotional management is found in our willingness to take personal responsibility for our feelings rather than simply blaming them on others. By this I mean that we are willing to honestly consider the lies in our own self talk that intensify the feelings we have and move them from negative emotions to destructive emotions. If we are willing to identify and challenge the lies about our worth as persons that underlie the feelings we have, we can begin to experience the freedom that comes from actually controlling our own emotions.

Managing our own emotions, however, does not mean that we will never feel bad. Living in a sin-cursed world in sin-cursed bodies we will experience bad circumstances that will produce the negative emotions of anger, hurt, and objective fear. Jesus was well acquainted with such emotions as a "man of sorrows, acquainted with grief". However, learning to manage our feelings like he did will help us to keep those negative emotions from slipping into the destructive and sinful emotions of hatred, self-pity, and anxiety. What keeps us from hating others is experiencing the love of God even while we are angry. What keeps us from throwing a pity party for ourselves is the joy of the Spirit experienced in the middle of our pain. What prevents us from becoming paralyzed with anxiety is the peace that passes all understanding even while we are afraid.

Exercises

1. Describe a recent situation in which your feelings were hurt by what someone said or did. What were you feeling at the time (anger, hurt, fear)? Note the natural tendency to blame that person for the way you were feeling to justify or rationalize your response to them. Now try to identify the false assumption you were telling yourself when you were

hurt by them. Note how much easier it is to blame them than identify your own false assumption.

2. Review this situation until you are able to verbalize the false assumption that is really hurting your feelings. The fact that you can blame the offensive person will seem more important than identifying your own false assumption (I will be worthy if they didn't treat me that way). Focus your attention on the false assumption rather than the offense and recognize that it is the lie about your worth as a person that intensifies your emotion. Specifically, the offense caused you to become angry, but the lie about your worth intensified your anger into hatred.

3. Fully acknowledge your feelings to God. If the situation you are remembering occurred more than 30 seconds ago, you are no longer dealing with anger, you are dealing with hatred. While it may be easily justified in your mind by reviewing how inappropriate or ugly the offense was, the resulting hatred will continue to fester within your soul and infect other relationships.

4. Be honest with God about the hatred you have inside for the one who hurt you. Express not only your hatred for the one who hurt you, but also all your justifications for why you hate them and rationalizations for what you intend to do to make it right. Confess the false assumptions discovered earlier (I will be worthy if this person had not said that or done this, etc.). Ask God to forgive you for your unbelief about your own worth and cleanse you from the hatred in your soul. Allow God to affirm your worth and convince you that you are secure in His love and significant in His plan.

5. Because you choose to believe that you are worthy regardless of what that person said or did to you, commit yourself to be used of God to love others despite your feelings. Rejecting the natural tendency to dwell on the offense, be willing to be used of God to love and minister to others around you. As

you focus your attention on acting responsible as a worthy child of God, you will notice that your hurt feelings fade away and are replaced with the love, joy, and peace we sometimes call serenity .

4. Behavioral Redirection

Learning the personal skills of cognitive restructuring and emotional management are necessary steps to behavioral redirection. The emotions we feel are important indicators of whether or not we believe the gospel for ourselves. When our thinking is correct according to the gospel, our feelings are radically different than when we are caught up in the never ending cycle of frustration shown in the Solomon Syndrome as taught in the Alpha Series.

Our natural false assumptions about what we need to be worthy (i.e. secure and significant as persons) establish a variety of false goals in our personal and relational lives. For instance, if my false assumption is, "I will be worthy if I can meet my wife's expectations", then my false goal is to do or say the things I think will make her happy. Obviously, there is nothing false about making my wife happy, but when I believe that my worth as a person depends on my performance and her approval, the goal of meeting her expectations becomes false. What makes any goal a false goal is not the goal itself, but the false assumptions that underlie that goal.

As long as I am able to reach my false goal (meet my wife's expectations), she is happy and I enjoy a temporary sense of satisfaction as a person. But when I am unable or unwilling to meet her expectations I get frustrated. Whenever we are blocked from reaching a false goal we naturally feel frustrated and typically try a little harder. Repeated failure to reach our false goals intensifies our frustration to the point that we may tend to deny or even break with reality just to compensate for the emotional pain we experience.

Virtually all false goals sooner or later lead to intense frustration if they are not met. The good news, however, is that every false goal can be turned into a true goal of ministry if we are willing to do the cognitive restructuring and emotional management discussed earlier. Believing I am worthy because of who God has made me to be allows me to strive for the true goal of ministering to my wife rather than simply making her happy by meeting her expectations. My own faith in the gospel frees me to actually care about and love my wife like Christ.

Although the true goal of ministry (i.e. loving my wife like Christ) may also be blocked just like the false goals, the emotions I feel will be radically different. Instead of the natural hatred and bitterness I will experience anger mixed with love. Instead of self pity and despair I will feel hurt mixed with joy. And rather than anxiety and worry I will feel concern mixed with peace. In short, I will experience the negative emotions rather than the sinful and destructive emotions. The frustration we feel when believing that our needs are not met is radically different from the feelings we have when striving for a true goal of ministry. As a result, our verbal and non-verbal behavior will reflect this difference and must be managed in order to relate to others in a consistent and healthy manner.

Ministry or Manipulation?

Behavioral redirection simply refers to a change in our verbal and non-verbal behavior from that which is unhealthy or dysfunctional to that which is healthy. We define healthy behavior as *ministry* or service to others and dysfunctional behavior as self-centered *manipulation*. The only difference between ministry and manipulation is *motive*. It is possible to do or say exactly the same things with completely different motives. I can buy my wife some flowers for two different reasons: to express my love to her, or to try to get something from her. The act is the same, but the motives are different. The key to behavioral redirection is the recognition of motives that underlie all behavior.

> The only difference between ministry and manipulation is *motive*.

Healthy behavior is what we do or say that is motivated by **faith** in our own worth according to the gospel; **hope** concerning our own needs for personal security and significance being consistently met; and genuine **love** for others. Unhealthy or dysfunctional behavior is what we say or do that is motivated by **fear** of failure and rejection; **guilt** over our own faults and failures; and **pride** in comparing ourselves to others. Behavior motivated by faith, hope and love is called ministry; that behavior motivated by fear, guilt, and pride is called manipulation.

> Behavior motivated by faith, hope and love is called ministry that behavior motivated by fear, guilt, and pride is called manipulation.

The personal skill of behavioral redirection requires the utmost honesty with God, others, and ourselves. We must first be willing to ask ourselves why we do what we do or say what we say. What is the true motivation for our verbal and non-verbal behavior? Is it really for the sake of loving and serving others? Or is it really for our own benefit?

All too often we seek to justify what we say or do by assuming that we are just trying to do what is best for others, especially in our own families. The dad who demands that his children "settle down" may say that he is looking out for their welfare, but may really want some peace and quiet for himself after a long day at work. The mom who berates her husband for not spending "quality time" with the kids may actually want a break for herself. Recognition of such self-centered behavior in the family or other social systems demands an honest examination of our own motives. Often the true motive for our behavior is the need to transfer guilt to others, in order to feel worthy ourselves. This is called blaming others for how I feel. Whenever we do this it is a sure sign we have forgotten our true worth in Christ.

Having discovered the natural tendency in ourselves to manipulate rather than minister, we must be willing to agree with God when we are falsely motivated and need to be changed. It is important to realize that we cannot really know our true motivation much less change it apart from divine intervention. We need to ask God to reveal

> We must be willing to agree with God when we are falsely motivated and need to be changed.

the motivation of our behavior and ask him to change our manipulation to ministry on a daily basis. Remember, manipulation is our natural motivation; ministry requires divine power.

Finally, we need to be honest with our family members and others about our motivation if we are really going to redirect our behavior. The only difference between ministry and manipulation is motive. All too often we seek to manipulate our spouse, children, or others under the guise of "doing what is best for them". Despite our best efforts to cover such selfish motivation, our family members frequently discern our manipulation tactics. When we find ourselves motivated by selfish concerns and trying to manipulate, we need to be honest with those family members and seek reconciliation.

Since it is possible to do or say the same things for two different motives, we need to focus our attention on *why* we do rather than *what* we do. Behavioral redirection means we redirect our behavior away from manipulation and control toward ministry and support. This requires setting true goals of ministry

> Since it is possible to do or say the same things for two different motives, we need to focus our attention on *why* we do rather than *what* we do.

rather than pursuing our natural desires.

A true goal of ministry may be defined as that which we can accomplish through divine help alone, apart from the cooperation of anyone else. For example, a husband may set a goal of expressing love for his wife regardless of her response to him or her behavior.

Through the personal leadership of the Spirit, that husband can say and do things that will express love regardless of how his wife is acting or responding to him. Reaching a true goal of ministry brings a greater sense of personal satisfaction than manipulating and controlling others. While this takes "mountain moving faith" to actually believe and practice, redirecting our behavior towards ministry rather than manipulation is really the only healthy way to live.

It is important to note here that we not only have a natural tendency to manipulate others, but are likely to be manipulated ourselves. As any parent can attest, manipulation is a primary tool for children to use in order to get their own way. Not every used car salesman really wants to "help" you. In fact, our world is filled with people who are in need of behavioral redirection and will, therefore, seek to manipulate you for their own advantage in any way possible.

Christianity has its fair share of manipulative con artists. Since Simon the magician tried to buy Peter's gift of healing, religious con artists have sought to manipulate people in a variety of ways. Generally, the game is presented as, "If you were really a good Christian, you would give me what I want." What makes it so easy to con religious people is their own motives of fear, guilt, and pride. Not believing the gospel for themselves, they naturally feel guilty and try to cover it up with prideful "good works". It is quicker and less messy to write a check or give some cash than it is to truly minister to such con artists. Likewise, the proverbial "TV evangelists" and other false teachers prey on the fearful, guilty, and proud motives in their audience to "fleece the flock". Paul warned the Ephesian elders of such "grievous wolves in sheep's clothing" who would seek to manipulate rather than minister to the flock. To the extent we are willing to develop the skill of behavioral redirection in ourselves we will also avoid being manipulated and learn to recognize the need in others. God reads our motives like an open book and is willing to change them as he conforms us to the image of his son.

Recognition of Motives

Behavioral redirection requires the supernatural ability to recognize the true nature of our motivations. The Bible contrasts a life falsely motivated by fear, guilt, and pride with that motivated by faith, hope, and love. A healthy lifestyle of grace is referred to as "walking in the light" or "walking in the Spirit". This lifestyle is in stark contrast with the legalistic or religious lifestyle the Bible describes as "walking in the vanity of our minds" or "walking after the flesh". The personal skill of behavioral redirection is the ability to change our motivation from fear, guilt, and pride (a lifestyle of law) to faith hope and love (a lifestyle of grace).

In 1 John 1:5-9 we are encouraged to "walk in the light" which is essentially the same thing as walking in the Spirit. John promises that if we walk in the light we will have fellowship with God (who is himself, light) and the blood of Jesus Christ will continuously cleanse us from all sins. Regarding our motivations, this promise assures us that "walking in the light" guarantees the elimination of fear, guilt, and pride. But what does it mean to walk in the light as He (God) is in the light? From the context it is clear that John is referring to our being able to see things the way they really are…especially how we see ourselves. Naturally we have a tendency to identify ourselves with the flesh (a biblical term for the worthless and sinful person we were born into this world as and have been trying hard to clean up). According to the gospel of grace, however, all believers are created in Christ Jesus, holy and without blame before the Father. Therefore, to view ourselves as God sees us means that we distinguish our real selves from our flesh. In other words, we must recognize that we are a brand new person with the righteousness of Christ while at the same time fully acknowledging the existence of the self-centered flesh. Although we have been spiritually transformed into the image of Christ, we yet live our new lives in the same old physical body that still houses the selfish and sinful nature called the flesh. Until our redemption is complete with a new body to match our new identity, we will continue to experience the innate conflict between who we really are and how we behave ourselves in this world.

Paul describes this conflict in his own personal testimony recorded in Romans 7: 14 ff. There he not only makes the distinction between his new identity in Christ and his sinful nature or flesh, but also makes it clear that we have no power to rid ourselves of the influence, actions, or motives of the flesh. He laments his confusion about his own behavior saying the things he wanted to do, he couldn't and the things he didn't want to do, he did. Clearly, Paul was in agony referring to himself as a "wretched man" in need of deliverance. In addition to choosing to believe we are not our flesh despite its presence in our earthly experience, we must also believe that only God, through Jesus Christ, by means of the indwelling Spirit can rid us of our fleshly motivations.

> In addition to choosing to believe we are not our flesh despite its presence in our earthly experience, we must also believe that only God, through Jesus Christ, by means of the indwelling Spirit can rid us of our fleshly motivations.

The need for behavioral redirection is apparent from the fact that even those behaviors we consider to be good may be improperly motivated. In that great "love" chapter, 1 Corinthians 13, Paul provides us with a list of good behaviors that mean nothing unless motivated by the love of God. Whatever we say or do, regardless how religious it may seem, is useless and empty if it is improperly motivated. As far as God is concerned, it's not what we do or say that counts, but why we say it or do it. He doesn't judge according to outward appearances, but according to the motives of the heart.

In fact, the basis of our rewards at the judgment seat of Christ is said to be our motivation.

In 1 Corinthians 3 Paul warns us to take heed of how we build on the foundation of Christ, seeing that every man's work will be judged "of what sort it is". That which is built of "wood, hay, and stubble" will be burned; and that which is built of "gold, silver, and precious stones" will be rewarded. These "building materials" represent the opposite motivations of our behavior. "Wood, hay, and stubble" may be viewed as the motives of fear, guilt, and pride, while "gold, silver, and precious stones" represents the motives of faith, hope, and love. Note again that what we say or do can be motivated by either set. In fact, both sets of motivations are working within at any given time since the flesh with its motivations of fear, guilt, and pride continuously opposes the new persons God has made us to be motivated by faith, hope, and love. Virtually all our behavior, both verbal and non-verbal, is motivated by either the flesh or the Spirit. The transformation from one to the other is what is meant by behavioral redirection. Like cognitive restructuring and emotional management this personal skill is vital to our being able to love others like Christ. As we become skilled in changing our core motivations we are able to move from manipulation to true ministry. The rewards for such a change are many on both the personal and relational level.

The Miracle of Change

It is important to note at this point that while the need to change our motivation from fear, guilt, and pride in a legalistic lifestyle to faith, hope, and love in a lifestyle of grace, such a change cannot be accomplished in our own strength. As will be more fully explained in the next chapter, such a fundamental change requires the comfort, direction, and power of the indwelling Holy Spirit. As always, our responsibility in this matter is to exercise faith... God's responsibility is the power to get it done. In 2 Corinthians 3:18 we are given an overview of how change takes place. As we focus on our new identity in Christ we are miraculously changed into the same image by the Spirit of God. This process is developmental (we are changed from glory to glory) and is accomplished entirely by the power of the

> *2 Corinthians 3:18*
> But we all, with *our* face having been unveiled, having beheld the glory of the Lord as in a mirror, are being changed into the same image from glory to glory, even as by the Lord Spirit.

Spirit. Our responsibility in the matter is to focus on our new identity in Christ by faith…God's responsibility is to do the changing.

The same concept is revealed in 1 John where we are encouraged to walk in the light. As mentioned earlier, walking in the light

> **To walk in the light, then, demands that we recognize our heavenly position as well as our earthly condition.**

is a matter of seeing ourselves in the same light God does. This means that we view ourselves as brand new spirit beings who are continually motivated in all we say or do by faith, hope, and love. This new identity, however, still lives in the same old body we were born with so that we must also see ourselves as yet possessing the flesh motivated by fear, guilt, and pride. To walk in the light, then, demands that we recognize our heavenly position as well as our earthly condition. Our heavenly position in Christ means that we are properly motivated, whereas our earthly condition means that we also have the motives of the flesh. John goes on to explain that if we say we have no sin (the flesh), we deceive ourselves. So long as we live on this earth in these bodies we will have the flesh to contend with daily. But if we confess our sins (agree with God concerning our fleshly motives), He (God) is faithful (consistent) and just (fair) to forgive (send it away) and to cleanse us. In other words, when we exercise the faith necessary to see ourselves as God sees us, God changes our motives from fear to faith, from guilt to hope, and from pride to love. This is true behavioral redirection from the inside out.

Breaking the Hurt-Hate-Hurt Cycle

Nowhere is the need for behavioral redirection any greater than in breaking the hurt-hate-hurt cycle within the family system. The prideful response to those who disappoint us, much less abuse us in some way, is to hate; and that hate motivates us to hurt others in return. Abused children often grow up to abuse their children because this vicious cycle has never been broken. Those who are hurt by others will hate, and those who hate will hurt others. Behavioral redirection almost always involves a conscious choice to break this deadly cycle of hurt and hate with the power of forgiveness.

When we are disappointed or hurt by others we naturally react with resentment, bitterness and hatred. In our efforts to cope with such wounds we often simply repress the memories and all the emotions that were produced at the time we were wounded. Although we may be able to "go on with our lives" on the surface, deep inside our souls an abscess of hatred begins to form. It is those pockets of hatred inside that produce symptoms of personal dysfunction and relational problems. Unless we take the time to honestly examine ourselves, and face the painful memories that produced the hatred inside, we can never "enter into life" as Jesus said.

The actual process of eliminating the internal hatred that leads us to hurting others is best described by the biblical concept of forgiveness. When we find ourselves hating those who have disappointed or abused us in some way, we must first admit that our flesh naturally responds with hate. Getting honest with ourselves and God about our hatred is really all the Bible requires for cleansing. We need to recognize that our hatred toward others who have hurt us (including ourselves and God) is as much a sin as the wrongs that we have suffered. While it is true others were at fault for wounding us in some way, we must realize hating them is never justified in God's eyes. Our fleshly response of hatred toward the offender will continue to destroy our lives long after the offense has ceased.

If anyone had a right to hate those who abused him, it was Jesus. Yet, during his crucifixion, Jesus prayed, "Father forgive them." For us to do anything less than forgive those who wound us is ultimately dysfunctional. However, we cannot give what we do not have. It is absolutely impossible for us to forgive others unless we know we have received forgiveness ourselves. "But, why do I need forgiveness?" we might say to ourselves. "I am the victim here, others are the offenders!" We need forgiveness for the hatred we have in our souls for others who offend us. When we confess our hatred to God, he is faithful (every time) and just (because he has already paid the penalty) to remind us of our forgiveness, and cleanse us from perceived guilt (1 John 1:9). Then, and, only then, when we realize we already have been forgiven in our unworthy condition, are we truly able to forgive others who trespass against us. Then, and only then, are we able to move from hatred to love for those who hurt us.

Summary

The personal skill of behavioral redirection is vital to relational empowerment. Loving others is not merely a set of good behaviors that we may choose to learn and practice. Loving others like Christ is far more than trying to develop and maintain good manners and live up to a moral code that is acceptable to God and others. Loving others requires the supernatural work of the indwelling Spirit elimi-

> Loving others like Christ is far more than trying to develop and maintain good manners and live up to a moral code that is acceptable to God and others.

nating the self-centered nature of the flesh and imparting to us the character of God in the new persons he has made us to be. When we are willing to check the motives behind all that we do or say and trust God to use us to love others in his power, the miracle of change takes place and our behavior is redirected. The kind of love we are called to is God's love. It is unconditional, sacrificial, initiating, eternal, and intelligent. Such divine love cannot be developed through natural human means, but must be worked in us supernaturally by the Spirit of God. Miraculously changing us from self-centered takers to loving givers is the beginning of the relational empowerment needed to live out the gospel of grace in a recovering lifestyle.

Exercises

1. The most challenging task in developing the skill of behavioral redirection is to come to grips with the existence of our own false motives. Describe one "good" behavior in your every day routine and note how you may be motivated differently even though it is the same behavior. (hint: ask what you said or did, and then ask why you said or did it)

2. When we are honest with ourselves we might be somewhat shocked to see how much of our behavior is motivated out of fear, guilt, or pride. Rather than spend time justifying or condemning yourself review what God says he has done to make you a brand new person even though you may not act like it. Write out Ephesians 1: 3-9 and substitute your name for the pronouns "us", "we", etc.

3. Behavior motivated by fear, guilt, or pride is not only manipulative and self centered, but ultimately undermines our relationships to others. Recognizing the difference between the new person God has made you to be and your dysfunc-

tional flesh, describe in detail three (3) situations in which your flesh acted selfishly out of fear, guilt, and pride.

4. Realizing the subtle sinfulness of our flesh is just as important as believing how righteous God has made us to be. Review the three situations listed above and note the profound difference between the righteous person God has made you to be in Christ and the total selfishness of your dysfunctional flesh. When you can see both you are walking in the light.

5   While walking in the light take a few moments to tell God what you see, especially the depravity of your own fleshly motivations. Rejoicing in the truth that you are not your flesh, ask God to forgive your sins and cleanse you from your flesh. Count on him to do this work in you every time you confess your need, and thank him for paying the price for you with the blood of his own son.

5. Spiritual Enlightenment

Among the personal skills required for relational empowerment, perhaps the most important is that of spiritual enlightenment. The skills of cognitive restructuring, emotional management, and behavioral redirection all depend on the supernatural work of the Holy Spirit to change our thinking, our feelings, and our motives respectively. In a sense, the skill of spiritual enlightenment is involved in all three of the other personal skills and, therefore, may be seen, on one level at least, as the most vital.

What Is Spiritual Enlightenment?

By spiritual enlightenment we mean the experience and understanding of how God continually works in and through us as well as his presence and activities in the world. Specifically, we are concerned with our own personal relationship with him through the Holy Spirit. On the night before he was crucified Jesus met with his disciples to prepare them not only for his arrest, trial, and crucifixion; but also for their ministry following his resurrection. He shocked them by announcing that he was leaving them, but promised them that he would send them another comforter whom he called the Spirit of Truth. It was there he also gave them a new commandment to love others like he loved them in his absence. It is worth noting the link between Jesus' calling them to love one another and his promise of the indwelling of the Holy Spirit he called the "Comforter". The only way we can truly love others like Christ is through the leadership and power of the Spirit. Whatever relational empowerment we may need to be able to love others is possible only by the work of the Holy Spirit in our lives.

Spiritual enlightenment is the understanding and insights provided by the Comforter according to the promises of Jesus to his disciples. Such enlightenment is needed for us to practice the other three personal skills. It is the Spirit of God that enables us to identify our false assumptions and replace them with biblical assumptions of our worth as persons. It is the Spirit in his role as the Comforter who miraculously keeps our negative emotions from becoming sinful and destructive. And, finally, it is the Spirit who exposes our natural selfishness and motivates us with faith, hope, and love.

In his letter to the Ephesians Paul prayed for believers to have the spiritual enlightenment we so desperately need. In Ephesians 1:17-19 he prayed, *"That the God of our Lord Jesus Christ, the Father of glory, may give unto you the spirit of wisdom and revelation in the knowledge of him: The eyes of your understanding being enlightened; that you may know what is the hope of his calling, and what the riches of glory of his inheritance in the saints, And what is the exceeding greatness of his power..."* Spiritual enlightenment is here described as God's gift of wisdom and revelation so that we can recognize the hope we have in his calling us, appreciate the riches of our blessing him, and realize the resurrection power of Christ. In short, spiritual enlightenment is the work God does in our minds and hearts to not only comfort us but also lead, guide, direct, remind, assure, and empower us.

> Ephesians 1:17-19
> That the God of our Lord Jesus Christ, the Father of glory, may give unto you the spirit of wisdom and revelation in the knowledge of him: The eyes of your understanding being enlightened; that you may know what is the hope of his calling, and what the riches of glory of his inheritance in the saints, And what is the exceeding greatness of his power...

As a personal skill, spiritual enlightenment may be thought of as the ability to recognize and rely upon God in coping with the issues of everyday life. As noted above we cannot even recognize the lies about our personal worth without the understanding and insights given to us by the Spirit. We must learn to rely upon the indwelling Spirit to teach us, lead us, remind us, and guide us into all truth about our true identity in Christ and how that meets our personal needs. But understanding and insight into our problem cannot, by itself, solve the problem or effect the needed change. Realizing we have a problem and recognizing the need to change is important, but true change involves a "spiritual awakening" centered on the fact that God does for us (through his indwelling Spirit) what we could not do for ourselves. Spiritual enlightenment, then, not only reveals our need for change, but also is the means by which that change occurs. Both the *need* to change our thinking, feeling, and behavior and the *ability* to change are included in the concept of spiritual enlightenment.

The Promise of the Spirit

Much can be learned about spiritual enlightenment by reviewing the biblical promises concerning the work of the Holy Spirit in our lives. As mentioned earlier, Jesus sought to comfort and instruct his worried disciples by promising them that he would not leave them comfortless (literally, like orphans) but would come to them through his Spirit. The various names for the Holy Spirit reveal some of the things Jesus promised he would do. For instance, Jesus called him the Comforter implying that his central task is to comfort us as we live and love in this sin cursed world. Although spiritual enlightenment often involves some sort of suffering, it is important to realize that suffering will occur whether or not we become enlightened in the process. All of us must suffer due to the fact that we continue to live in a sin-cursed world that is falling apart, in sin-cursed bodies that are also falling apart.

The connection to developing the personal skill of spiritual enlightenment is simply the fact that God uses such times of suffering for our benefit. This is what the writer of Hebrews called "chastening" which he says God does for all his loved ones that they might enjoy the "peaceable fruit of righteousness". A primary role of the indwelling Spirit of God is to comfort us in all our times of suffering. This he does by giving us personal assurance through his own leadership and control in our everyday lives.

What made Jesus so healthy and able to function so well in this world? It was the personal assurance and leadership of the Holy Spirit we are referring to as spiritual enlightenment. Beginning with His conception in Mary's womb, and through His resurrection from the tomb, Jesus was empowered by the Spirit of God to say and do all things necessary to fulfill the Father's plan for his life. It was the miraculous and supernatural working of the Holy Spirit, in and through Him, that enabled Jesus to complete His ministry in this world.

How does this apply to us? Remember, everything that is true of Jesus is true of you. Look at Paul's experience. After describing his agonizing struggle with indwelling sin in Romans 7, Paul reveals the marvelous way that God provides for our deliverance from the habit and power of sin and dysfunction through the work of the Holy Spirit (Romans 8). We are under no condemnation, have the mind of Christ, and are fully equipped with resurrection power. The mind and power of the Holy Spirit that influenced and led Paul is in each of us as well. This same Spirit that assured and led Jesus and Paul now lives in all who accept Jesus as their personal savior.

> Jesus promised that the Holy Spirit would personally lead us, continually teach us, and constantly remind us of all that Jesus said and did.

In addition to his work of comforting us and guiding us into all truth, Jesus promised that the Holy Spirit would personally lead us, continually teach us, and constantly remind us of all that Jesus said and did.

Finally, he promised that the Spirit would not speak of himself, but that he would glorify Jesus instead; meaning that the Holy Spirit would make Jesus real to us in our own unique lives. The heart of spiritual enlightenment, then, not only involves the much needed understanding of ourselves and insights into our purpose in this life, but also the realization of our potential to fulfill our "high calling of God in Christ Jesus" as we learn to love others the way Christ loves us. It is what may be referred to as Christ-actualization or, simply, the privilege of being Christ to others.

The Leadership of the Spirit

Just as Jesus was led by the Spirit in all that he did or said during his earthly ministry, so also are believers personally led by the same Spirit. Learning to depend on this personal leadership in all issues of our everyday lives is an essential component of spiritual enlightenment. In Romans 8:14-17, Paul describes the personal assurance each one of us may receive from the indwelling Spirit of God. He begins by the simple statement that "as many as are led by the Spirit of God, they are the sons of God," (verse 14), meaning the "adult children of God" are the ones led by the Spirit. The use of the Greek term "huios" (sons) indicates that believers are not to relate to God as immature and helpless babes, but as full grown adult children and heirs. All who follow the personal leadership of the indwelling Spirit will relate to God as adult children and heirs to the kingdom. They are motivated by faith, hope, and love (a life-

> **Romans 8:14-17**
> For as many as are led by *the* Spirit of God, they are the sons of God.
> For you have not received the spirit of bondage again to fear, but you have received the Spirit of adoption by which we cry, Abba, Father!
> The Spirit Himself bears witness with our spirit that we are the children of God.
> And if we are children, then we are heirs; heirs of God and joint-heirs with Christ; so that if we suffer with *Him*, we may also be glorified together.

style of grace) rather than the fear, guilt, and pride of an external set of rules and regulations (the law). They are motivated by knowing who they are, where they stand, and the glory they have in Christ. By equating the personal leadership of the Holy Spirit with the adult-child status, Paul implies we live and act like adult children of God because we have been given the Spirit of His Son who leads us to know and accept our status with the mind of Christ.

Since our conduct cannot be controlled by the law, (an external set of rules and regulations), we must be governed internally by grace through the personal leadership of the Holy Spirit. This very thing God promises to do for all who receive His son Jesus as their personal savior. But how do we know He is leading us? Can we really trust Him in all areas of our lives? These and many other questions tend to cause us to doubt the reality of being led by the Spirit, so Paul assures us in these verses that we are, in fact, being led by the Spirit.

The personal leadership of the Spirit may best be understood in terms of our ability to hear God talking to us. Jesus said, "My sheep hear my voice, and I know them, and they follow me..." (John 10:27). Hearing the voice of Jesus is necessary to follow His leadership. It is for this very reason that He promises that He would not leave us comfortless in this world, but would come to us through His Spirit living within (John 14:16-18).

Three factors need to be considered when trying to understand the way we hear from God. First, we must realize that since God has given us the ability to think, He will naturally speak to us in the privacy of our own hearts or minds. As the prophet Elijah noted, it is not in the loudness of

UNDERSTANDING HOW WE HEAR FROM GOD
1. Persistent thoughts.
2. The filter of scripture.
3. Our circumstances
All interpreted through faith.

cataclysmic events, but rather the still small voice within that we shall hear God. The voice of God through the indwelling Spirit will frequently appear in a spontaneous flow of persistent thoughts in our minds. This does not rule out the possibility of a neon sign in the sky, or a thunderous roar like the ocean, but most likely it will be a persistent thought repeated over and over in our minds.

Persistent thoughts, however, are not enough to really discern the voice of Jesus. It is quite possible to have persistent thoughts in our minds that are not of God, as in the case of certain obsessions. This underscores the necessity for filtering our thoughts through the written Word of God, the Bible. This miraculous book was inspired and preserved by God so that we might be aware of how he speaks to us, and what he is concerned about in general. The same Spirit who inspired the forty different men to write the various books and letters of the Bible over a period of 1600 years, will also guide each reader into a proper understanding and personal application of the scriptures. Thus, the written Word of God should be used as a safeguard against the thoughts and intents of the heart that are opposed to God, (Hebrews 4:12).

Circumstances also play a role in hearing God's voice, and following the leadership of the Spirit. Whatever God leads us to do; He will arrange the circumstances of our lives to accommodate His will. For the believer, nothing is left to chance, or is simply a coincidence. Although it's much easier to look back on the circumstances of our lives, and see how God has led us (hindsight is always 20/20), we may be assured that He is continually "ordering the steps of the righteous." Our own thoughts, and the written Word of God, combined with our circumstances in life constitute the main factors we need to consider in determining God's leadership. However, these three factors alone cannot truly reveal

> Our own thoughts and the written Word of God, combined with our circumstances in life constitute the main factors we need to consider in determining God's leadership.

God's voice, and leadership in our lives. The bottom line in this issue, as with all others in the Christian life, is FAITH. "But without faith it is impossible to please Him: for he that cometh to God must believe that He is, and that he is a rewarder of them that diligently seek him" (Hebrews 11:6). In hearing God's voice, or following His leadership, we must trust (1) that God exists, and (2) that God is speaking to us, and will lead us. Only when we believe that God is leading us will we be able to follow His leadership.

Besides the failure to trust that God really is leading us, another great obstacle stands in our way of hearing His voice...our fear. *Often we are afraid of what God might say to us if He did speak to us personally.* While the "fear of God" is healthy in the sense that we reverence Him, and are willing to submit ourselves to Him completely, being "afraid of God" is really an expression of unbelief in God's goodness and infinite love for us. To assure us on this point, Paul reveals that we have not received "the spirit of bondage" again to fear, but the Spirit of adoption (Romans 8:15).

> Being "afraid of God" is really an expression of unbelief in God's goodness and infinite love for us.

The "spirit of adoption" is the legal privilege we may enjoy because we are legally adopted into God's family, one with God's only begotten Son, Jesus. Far from being something to be feared, such personal leadership of the "Spirit of adoption" is a fantastic opportunity for all who will receive it by faith. To be led and empowered like Jesus is the way we truly experience the benefits of being in God's family.

Paul tells us that the Holy Spirit's first and greatest job as the Spirit of adoption is to assure us that we are the children of God. Personally, this means that the Holy Spirit is continually leading us to the knowledge and experience of our new life in Christ with all its security and significance. Because we are the children of God, we are "heirs of God" and "joint heirs with Christ." Every day the Holy Spirit will be speaking to us in our minds, through his written

Word and in our circumstances to assure us that we are the adopted children of God who can never be disinherited, and will inherit all the blessings of God in Christ. To the extent that we first hear we are worthy heirs of God, we are in a position to receive instruction on what we ought to do, and the power to do it. The Spirit of adoption will always teach us who we are in Christ, assure us in our new relationship to God as heirs, and then show us how to be Christ to others.

The Fullness of the Spirit

Another aspect of spiritual enlightenment may be summarized by the biblical concept known as being filled with the Spirit. In Ephesians 5:18, we are given the command, "and be not drunk with wine, wherein is excess; but be filled with the Spirit." It is written in the indicative mood so that we realize that being filled with the Spirit is not an option, but a command. It is written in the present tense so that we understand that being filled with the Spirit is to be a continuous experience as opposed to an occasional or weekly experience of a "religious high." It is also written in the passive voice so that we realize it is not something we may do to ourselves, but rather something that is done to us. Finally, the analogy of being drunk with wine reveals that the filling of the Spirit is a matter of control over our lives. When we choose to believe the Holy Spirit lives within us, and are willing to trust His leadership, we allow ourselves to be controlled by, or "filled" with the Spirit. The fullness of the Spirit, then, is not that we get more of the Spirit than we had before, but that the Spirit has more control in our lives. The skill of spiritual enlightenment, then, is really a matter of allowing the Holy Spirit to control our lives on a daily basis.

> Ephesians 5:18
> "And be not drunk with wine, wherein is excess; but be filled with the Spirit."

Three other scriptures reveal more specifically how this is done. In Ephesians 4:30, we are told literally to "stop grieving the Spirit", in 1 Thessalonians 5:19, we are commanded to "stop quenching the Spirit", and in Galatians 5:16 we are told to "keep on walking in the Spirit". Allowing the Spirit to control our lives begins with letting go of our own control and getting out of the way of the Spirit. Developing the personal skill of spiritual enlightenment, then, involves a daily practice of letting go of control and depending on the leadership and power of the Spirit of God.

But how do we, "Let go and let God" as some have put it? What is involved in this daily practice of spiritual enlightenment? From the time we are born into this world we have a natural desire to control and manipulate people and circumstances to meet our own needs and fulfill our own plans. Operating under the natural assumptions that we know what is best for ourselves and others, we naturally devise our plans to make it happen. We grieve the Spirit when we follow our own plans and ideas rather than listen to, and follow the Spirit. This is why Paul tells us literally to, "Stop grieving the Spirit". When you command someone to stop doing something, it is implied that they are in the process of doing it already. By his command to stop grieving the Spirit Paul implies that our natural tendency is to grieve him by following our own plan for our lives. To allow the Spirit to have control (be filled with the Spirit) we are going to have to quit controlling our lives ourselves.

Likewise, we quench the Spirit when we listen to the advice of others without consulting the Spirit. Have you noticed how other people are quick to devise a plan for your life? They seem to know what is best for you and are sometimes quick to tell you what you ought to do in any given situation. In addition, we often seek the advice of others when we are faced with difficult decisions. We consult books, go online, or ask our friends and family for their opinion. Seeking advice from others, in itself is generally useful, but following that advice without consulting God is dangerous. No matter how well meaning and insightful the opinion of man, it is still based on human knowledge and wisdom. Nothing can take the place of the divine wisdom of God. To practice spiritual enlightenment we will have to quit basing our decisions on the opinion of man alone...stop quenching the Spirit.

Instead of naturally grieving or quenching the Spirit we are admonished to "walk in the Spirit" by relying upon Him to personally lead us in all that we do or say. This does not mean that we cannot consider our own ideas or thoughts, neither does it mean we cannot hear from others; it simply means that we trust the Spirit to lead us personally, and rely upon His assurance, and comfort every day of our lives. Like the concept of "hearing God" walking in the Spirit requires the exercise of faith. We must believe that he wants to control our lives for our own good and that he will direct us personally in all our decisions. The spiritual enlightenment that comes from allowing the Spirit to control our lives is really the only reasonable way to live. It is a healthy and exciting lifestyle that empowers us to relate to others just like Christ.

The Renewing of the Mind

Of special significance when it comes developing the skill of spiritual enlightenment is what the Bible refers to as the "renewing of the mind". As noted earlier, if we are going to live a healthy functional life, we must learn to base our worth as persons on biblical assumptions of truth. These are composed of perceptions, thoughts and beliefs that coincide with the "mind of Christ" as opposed to our natural or "carnal mind". We are assured from the scriptures that we have the mind of Christ (1 Corinthians 2:14) and admonished to put it to use (Philippians 2:5). Because our feelings and behavior ultimately originate in our mind we must learn to perceive and think like Christ in order for our behavior to conform to our true identity.

The renewing of our minds by the indwelling Spirit is the key ingredient to spiritual enlightenment and involves all the work discussed above in the leadership and fullness of the Spirit. In

Romans 12: 1, 2 Paul counsels believers to "...present your bodies a living sacrifice, holy acceptable unto God..." and tells us how to do that by refusing to allow ourselves to be pressed into the mold (natural conditioning) of this world by allowing ourselves to be "...transformed by the renewing of your mind..." Likewise, in Ephesians 4: 17-24 he counsels us to put off the lifestyle of the old person we were and "be renewed in the spirit of your mind" so that we may put on the new lifestyle of righteousness and true holiness. The skill of personal enlightenment, then, is really a matter of allowing the Holy Spirit to renew our natural, self centered and dysfunctional mind.

It is important that we view the renewing of our minds as an ongoing process rather than an event. Even though being born again may be seen as an event in one point of time in our life, the renewing of our mind by the same Spirit that gave us eternal life is really a process that continues the rest of our lives. The analogy of physical growth and development used in the Bible to describe our spiritual development suggests that our minds will be renewed over time as opposed to instantly. Thus, the renewing of the mind will be a daily process.

Our part in the renewing of our mind is similar to what we have discussed in regards to the fullness and leadership of the Spirit. It may best be described as a willingness to allow the Spirit to change our thinking, feelings, and motivations. Perhaps the best example of that willingness is found in the psalm of repentance written by King David following his failure and sins in the Bathsheba affair (Psalm 51). The essence of his willingness to allow the Spirit to renew his mind is recorded in verses 10-12, *"Create in me a clean heart, O God; and renew a right spirit within me. Cast me not away from thy presence; and take not thy Holy Spirit from me. Restore unto me the joy of thy salvation; and uphold me with thy free spirit."* In this psalm David demonstrates, not only willingness, but a desperate cry to have God change him from the inside out. He fully acknowledged his need to be changed and recognized that only God could truly transform him completely.

The miracle of change sought by David after his sin is the renewing of the mind that yields the same inner change and transformation described by Paul in 2 Corinthians 3:18, *"But we all, with open face beholding as in a glass the glory of the Lord, are changed into the same image from glory to glory, even as by the Spirit of the Lord."* But here we are given a little more insight into our role in that change. What Paul means by the phrase, "with open face beholding as in a glass the glory of the Lord" is our honestly and continuously looking into the Bible (the glass or mirror) in order to see who we really are. The Bible is not a rule book to be studied so we can figure out what we have to do to change ourselves, but a revelation of what God has already done to make us brand new persons. Paul tells us what we see when we look into the glass or mirror... we see ourselves in Jesus!

By continually seeing ourselves in Christ we are changed (passive voice in the Greek) into the same image! That is we are made to be like Christ by believing what the Bible reveals about our new identity in Christ. The phrase, "from glory to glory" reminds us that this transformation is not an instantaneous event, but a developmental process. Our part, then, is to exercise faith in what the Word of God says about our new identity in Christ and allow the Spirit to renew our minds and change us from the inside out. Rather than worry and fret over how we are going to change ourselves and complain that it is too difficult, we simply choose to believe what God said he has done to make us brand new persons. It is the exercise of this simple, child-like faith in our new identity in Christ that gives us "access into the grace wherein we stand" and allows us to, "rejoice in the hope of the glory of God". Our part is to want to believe what God says he has done for us, the Spirit's part is to make it real to us. This process is the spiritual enlightenment we so desperately need to prepare ourselves to love others the way Jesus does.

Summary

Spiritual enlightenment is the greatest privilege we as believers may enjoy this side of heaven. To be personally comforted, led, taught, and empowered by the Spirit of God not only prepares us for our ministry to others, but also empowers us as we serve. Like the other personal skills, spiritual enlightenment is developed as we mature in the Lord. At first, we may find it difficult to recognize God working in and through us. Some go so far as to deny that he ever really does. Most of the difficulty lies in the fact that we yet posses a carnal (natural) mind that has been conditioned by trying to get on with life apart from God. We have learned to trust in our own knowledge of good and evil to manipulate people and things in our world in a religious self-effort to make ourselves secure and significant.

As a result, we naturally find ourselves "walking in darkness" or "walking after the flesh" and are not only empty and miserable ourselves, but also incapable of relating in a healthy way to others.

Spiritual enlightenment means that we learn to "walk in the light" or "walk after the Spirit" so that we hear God assure us of our security in his love and significance in his plan and are, therefore, free to actually care about and love others. Like Jesus, we learn to say what we hear the Father saying and do what we see the Father doing in the world around us. In essence, spiritual enlightenment is the experience of "being Christ" to others around us in our homes, on the job, or in the community. In this regard, spiritual enlighten-ment is more than understanding and insight...it is a lifestyle of victory and power in the grace of God.

Exercises

1. Describe your own experience in being "born again". How long was it before you began to worry about whether or not you were a "good Christian, or a Christian at all.

2. What, if anything, have you heard from God since you were born again? How has the Comforter assured you of your new identity in Christ?

3. Some people find it useful to practice "journaling" when trying to hear God's voice. This simply means spending time alone with God in prayer and writing down on paper what you think he is telling you. Try asking God what he thinks of you and who he has made you to be and write down the answers you receive.

4. Having heard God assure you of his love, ask him to lead you in loving others around you. (Note the way your sense of personal worth is enhanced is by being used of God to love others).

6. Spirituality Not Religiosity

At this juncture in our study of relational empowerment it is important to make a distinction between what we have just described as "spiritual enlightenment" and simply being religious. Many people get the two confused because of the natural, human tendency to equate spirituality and religiosity. To them, spirituality is simply a new lifestyle of religious activities such as church attendance, or membership and faithful involvement in a religious organization. Those who regularly engage in such religious activities or rituals are thought to be "spiritual" as opposed to those who do not.

Because of this confusion it is best to operationally define our terms. Religion may be defined as a system of rules and customs based on orthodoxy that is generally imposed on individuals who are born into the system and raised to obey its practices without question. It has a tendency to formalize, ritualize, and legalize individual experience and expression of spirituality; and is generally concerned with understanding and applying some form of spirituality to improve the human experience while also reinforcing the religious rules and customs.

> Religion may be defined as a system of rules and customs based on orthodoxy that is generally imposed on individuals who are born into the system and raised to obey its practices without question.

Spirituality, on the other hand, is more fundamental than the various religions that may grow out of it. It is highly personal, unique to the individual, experienced from within, and cannot be ex-

> Spirituality is highly personal, unique to the individual, experienced from within, and cannot be explained or contained in a system of rules and customs.

plained or contained in a system of rules and customs. It is rooted in the spiritual nature of the individual, not in the collective experience of the culture. At its core, spirituality is the recognition of a spiritual reality, the personal realization of that spiritual reality, and the expression of reverence for that which is spiritual.

Because spiritual enlightenment is so vital to relational empowerment, it should come as no surprise that the enemy would seek to undermine it with a counterfeit. In an effort to maintain our false identity in the flesh, the carnal mind immediately seeks to feign acceptability and, therefore, worth by turning all of its attention to becoming religious. It is all too happy to "dress itself up and take itself to church". There it can engage in its own plan of self improvement for its own glory. Remember, false assumptions of personal worth don't always look false! The evil thoughts of "I will be worthy if... can be completed with good looking religious activities such as church attendance, worship activities, and an outward compliance with a moral set of standards. The end result of such infantile thinking in the baby Christian is what Paul warned as "falling from grace". Such was the case for the Pharisees of Jesus day.

> In an effort to maintain our false identity in the flesh, the carnal mind immediately seeks to feign acceptability and, therefore, worth by turning all of its attention to becoming religious.

In this sense religion has always been the enemy of the cross of Christ. Biblical history records many examples of the terrible consequences of religiosity beginning with Cain murdering his brother, Abel. The fleshly attempt of Sarah and Abraham to fulfill the promise of God through their own natural means; the repeated failure of Israel as a nation to keep the law of Moses; the rejection and persecution of the prophets; and the continual opposition of the Pharisees to the grace and truth of Christ all illustrate the historical tendency toward and dangers of religiosity.

Satan being able to transform himself into an angel of light and his servants into ministers of the gospel demonstrates the deception of religiosity. His most subtle lies are based on "half-truths" that often sound religious and on the surface appear to be good. The "seducing spirits" Paul warns of in 2 Timothy are religious in nature suggesting that we may guarantee our worth as persons by a flurry of religious activities, emotional experiences, and intellectual insights. The blinding power of Satan always involves turning our attention away from the good news of all that God has done for us to focus on what we need to do, feel, or think to make ourselves worthy. This is the core of religiosity that literally denies the gospel and blasphemes the work of Christ on our behalf.

> Satan being able to transform himself into and angel of light and his servants into ministers of the gospel demonstrates the deception of religiosity.

As mentioned above, religiosity may be defined as a system of rules and customs based on orthodoxy. It is developed by the natural tendency to formalize, ritualize, and legalize individual experience and expression of spirituality. Those who are trapped in religiosity are generally concerned with understanding and applying some form of spirituality to improve the human experience, but are also compelled to reinforce the religious rules and customs they have developed. Maintenance of the rules and appearances becomes their top priority as opposed to trusting God and loving others. As a result, most of the historical crimes against humanity were committed in the name of religion (witness the period of crusades as well as the modern day jihads).

Spirituality, on the other hand is more fundamental than the various religions in that it is rooted in the spiritual nature of the individ-

> True spirituality cannot be explained or contained in a system of rules and customs because it originates in the spiritual nature of the individual, not in the collective experience of the culture.

ual. True spirituality cannot be explained or contained in a system of rules and customs because it originates in the spiritual nature of the individual, not in the collective experience of the culture. At its core it is the recognition of a spiritual reality, the personal realization of that spiritual reality, and the expression of reverence for that which is spiritual. By definition, then, spirituality is the result of an authentic and personal faith rather than a toxic faith.

Authentic Faith Verses Toxic Faith

Spiritual enlightenment, as we have defined it thus far, requires an authentic faith that is radically different from the toxic faith underlying the spiritual blindness of religiosity. It is helpful to contrast the two as to their origin, focus, and expression. Although such a contrast may seem a little "picky" if not too technical, the understanding of the difference between the two kinds of faith is essential if we are going to experience true spiritual enlightenment. In addition, both kinds of faith have a profound effect on our lives in general. Authentic faith will produce the hope we need to endure our circumstances and actually learn to love others, whereas toxic faith will lead to self centered behavior that destroys the lives of others.

As to its origin, authentic faith comes from within the individual by the exercise of their own freedom of choice *via love and forgiveness.* Toxic faith, on the other hand, is imposed on the individual from without, *via fear of rejection and shame.* It is impossible to create authentic faith in a person by coercion and threats, yet many religions employ a variety of "scare tactics" hoping to persuade others. The Bible makes it clear that authentic faith is a fruit of the in-

> Authentic faith:
> Comes from within.
>
> Toxic faith:
> Comes from without.

dwelling Spirit and reveals that it is the goodness of God that leads to repentance, not His threats.

The difference between the authentic faith needed for true spiritual enlightenment and the toxic faith that produces religiosity is clearly revealed by its focus. Authentic faith is focused on *divine provisions* to meet personal needs for worth. Toxic faith, however, is focused on *self-effort* to meet religious standards for acceptance and approval from God and others. Those who are caught up in a toxic faith will also be selfish and self centered because their focus is continually on their own efforts to look or feel good. Even though their selfishness may be cloaked in religious activities, they cannot help but worry about whether or not they are acceptable to God and especially to man. Authentic faith, on the other hand, is continually impressed with and amazed by what God has, is, and will do to satisfy our deepest needs. Attention is devoted to God's provisions for our well being rather than our own performance.

> **Authentic faith:**
> Is focused on *divine provisions* to meet personal needs for worth.
>
> **Toxic faith:**
> Is focused on *self-effort* to meet religious standards for acceptance and approval from God and others.

Finally, the most obvious difference between authentic faith and toxic faith is revealed in the expression of each. Authentic faith is continually expressed through *tolerance, acceptance, and compassion* for others no matter what the

> **Authentic faith:**
> Is the foundation for the spiritual enlightenment needed to love other like Christ.
>
> **Toxic faith:**
> Keeps us in the spiritual darkness and confusion that causes us to try to control and manipulate others.

circumstances. In strong contrast, toxic faith continually *seeks power and control to manipulate others and circumstances.* Because authentic faith is focused on divine provisions for our worth, it liberates us through spiritual enlightenment to be confident that our own needs have been and will continue to be met in what God has done for us. In that way authentic faith creates a genuine hope or joyful and confident expectation about our future. That hope not only gives us the endurance we need to persevere in our daily trials, but allows us to actually think about and love others.

The tragedy of a toxic faith is that it keeps us locked into a self-centered fear of rejection and failure, so that we experience constant guilt over our mistakes and often degenerates into an attitude of shame ("I am a mistake"). In such a condition we cannot possibly think about others unless it involves how we may control and manipulate them to satisfy our own needs. Authentic faith is the foundation for the spiritual enlightenment needed to love others like Christ; whereas toxic faith keeps us in the spiritual darkness and confusion that causes us to try to control and manipulate others. Healthy relationships can only be built on the expression of authentic faith through the spiritual enlightenment that it produces. Toxic faith ultimately destroys relationships as it prohibits the spiritual enlightenment needed to liberate us from our selfish flesh.

Toxic Faith and Religious Addiction

The consequences of exercising authentic faith or toxic faith are clearly seen in the kind of life that is produced. Authentic faith expressing itself in love will produce a healthy lifestyle of spiritual empowerment and love for others. Toxic faith will blind us to the comfort and power of the Spirit and produce a dysfunctional lifestyle filled with shattered dreams and littered with broken relationships.

Toxic faith typically leads to religious addiction which may be defined as using God, a church, or a belief system as an escape from reality, in an attempt to find or elevate a sense of self worth or well-being. Like all other addictions, the main symptom of religious addiction is denial. The woman who quotes Bible versus in every conversation and follows each statement with words like, "amen?", or "praise Jesus", or "hallelujah", usually thinks she is being "spiritual" and will surely be blessed by God for the way she talks. The man who faithfully attends every service of the church and "pays his tithes" rather than his bills, would likely defend his compulsion as being "on fire for Jesus" rather than admit his addiction. Such denial may even be expressed by statements such as, "I'm just getting high on Jesus" or "I'm hooked on God rather than drugs".

Some of the more common behaviors among religious addicts are: compulsive religious activity; laziness; giving to get; self-obsession; extreme intolerance; addiction to a religious high. Just as the alcoholic or drug addict uses chemicals to numb the personal pain, so the religious addict uses various rituals, dogma, or scripture texts and obsessive behaviors to find relief. Unfortunately there is often as much addiction in the "church house" as there is in the "crack house". Because the behaviors associated with religious addiction are often seen as "good" or as signs of "spirituality", however, the underlying motive and false assumptions go unchallenged.

In their book, "Toxic Faith", authors Stephen Arterburn and Jack Felton provide us with twenty-one beliefs of a toxic faith system. Their list may be broken down into three categories: 1. Religious performance, 2. Gaining approval from religious authority, and 3. Avoidance of any form of suffering. What makes these beliefs toxic is the foundational idea that our worth as persons depends on our own ability to please God rather than His grace in making us pleasing. In short, toxic faith and the religious addiction it produces is a natural consequence of failing to hear and apply the gospel of grace to our lives.

Not knowing that we have been made the righteousness of God in Christ leaves us to our own devices in trying to justify ourselves. Not realizing that the Father has sent forth the Spirit of His Son into our hearts leaves us trusting our own wisdom and knowledge of the law to make ourselves "good Christians". Not experiencing spiritual enlightenment concerning our own worth as persons leaves

> Not knowing that we have been made the righteousness of God in Christ leaves us to our own devices in trying to justify ourselves.

us stumbling around in the darkness of personal worthlessness. The root of religious addiction and all its dysfunction is the basic fear of failure and rejection that comes from viewing ourselves as naturally worthless, but trying to make ourselves worthy by our own efforts. This is not the healthy lifestyle promised by Jesus, but a very painful and unhealthy lifestyle filled with confusion, ignorance, and blindness.

Authentic Faith and Our Identity

How we answer the simple question, "Who am I?" determines the quality of our lives in many ways. What we believe about ourselves determines how we feel and ultimately how we act and relate to others. This is why the answer to any problem we may have must start with what the Bible calls the need to "renew" our minds with authentic rather than toxic faith.

> What we believe about ourselves determines how we feel and ultimately how we act and relate to others.

This is expressed by the apostle Paul in Ephesians 4:17, 18 where he warns Christians not to live like others "in the vanity of the mind". What is meant by the "vanity" of the mind is the personal emptiness explained in the following verses as being confused, ignorant, and blind concerning our own identity. We are naturally

> **Ephesians 4:17-18**
> This I say therefore, and testify in the Lord, that you should not walk from now on as other nations walk, in the vanity of their mind, having the understanding darkened, being alienated from the life of God through the ignorance that is in them, because of the blindness of their heart.

confused about who we really are, ignorant of how we got here and where we are going, and blind to the spiritual reality of our union with the divine. This is why spiritual enlightenment is so vital to a healthy, functional life.

Such a condition is extremely painful and sets the stage for all forms of addiction including religious addiction. Being confused, ignorant, and blind hurts us terribly. The best we can hope for naturally is a fleeting sense of satisfaction that temporarily covers a pervasive sense of emptiness. So intense is the personal suffering that it's only natural for us to become preoccupied with finding ways to feel better. We must find some way to "take the edge off". Our goal in life becomes to avoid pain and feel better each day. We are willing to give ourselves wholly to reaching that goal and set all other concerns aside in favor of that which we think will make us feel better about ourselves and our lives.

The addicted have a very low opinion of themselves even though it may be covered with multiple attempts to look good or feel good. They are usually trying very hard to prove their own worth as a person, but have deep feelings of insecurity and shame. On the surface they may appear to be quite religious and are determined to keep the moral code they have adopted. They may even compare themselves to others to prove their own superiority. But deep down inside they are plagued with a desperate fear of rejection by God and others. Often they are over-

> For many people the emotional relief they find in religious activities is as much a "high" as that of the drug addict or alcoholic.

whelmed by a sense of guilt and shame; and their pride desperately tries to cover their weaknesses by a flurry of religious good works. In such a state they are likely to be rude, obnoxious, or abusive towards others, even their own friends or family. Just as the alcoholic or drug addict uses chemicals to numb the personal pain, so the religious addict uses various rituals, dogma, scripture texts, and obsessive behaviors to find relief. For many people the emotional relief they find in religious activities is as much a "high" as that of the drug addict or alcoholic.

But Paul goes on in this text to remind us of a better way to live, "But ye have not so learned Christ; If so be that ye have heard him, and have been taught by him, as the truth is in Jesus" (Ephesians 4: 20-21). In contrast to the natural way we think of ourselves (essentially worthless, but trying hard to be better), he tells us to consider what we have learned from our relationship to Christ. Rather than see ourselves as the "old man" that is worthless and in need of reform, we have been taught to see ourselves as a "new man" that is perfect in Christ (created in righteousness and true holiness). What is needed to think this way about ourselves he refers to as being "renewed in the spirit of your mind", which implies the spiritual enlightenment that comes from authentic faith.

> **Ephesians 4:20-21**
>
> But ye have not so learned Christ; If so be that ye have heard him, and have been taught by him, as the truth is in Jesus

The foundational question of our true identity is at the heart of authentic faith. Rather than being coerced into believing in our own self effort to make ourselves acceptable to God and others, we may freely choose to believe all that God says he has done for us in Christ and focus on his provisions for our worth and well being. Choosing to believe in the divine provisions for our personal worth, we experience the hope of our deepest needs being met in Christ so that we are free to love and accept others. Those whose minds have been "renewed" to believe they are worthy apart from their own performance or the approval of others are not idle, but actively involved in serving one another in love. They too may go to church, read and study their Bibles, engage in various forms of worship, or be a member of some religious organization. But they do so because they know they are worthy out of a true heart of love and not in order to take away the pain of their own sense of worthlessness.

Am I Good or Bad?

Also at the core of the identity question is the need to understand ourselves as being essentially good or essentially bad. Philosophers, theologians, and more recently psychologists, sociologists, and anthropologists have long debated the issue of whether man is essentially good or bad. All religious systems seem to be divided into two camps on this question. There are those who believe that human beings are essentially good and focus on our innate dignity, while others see humanity as essentially evil and inherently bad. Depending on which camp we find ourselves in, we will naturally view ourselves as being either good or bad by nature. This fundamental view of ourselves is perhaps the single most important issue that determines a healthy identity. How we answer this question of our being essentially good or bad really determines how we will live and relate to others.

> How we answer this question of our being essentially good or bad really determines how we will live and relate to others.

In order to answer this question we must have some sort of standard, a "ruler" if you will, against which we may measure ourselves and determine whether we are good or bad. Erich Fromm describes religion as, "any group-shared system of thought and action that offers the individual a frame of orientation and an object of devotion". This description lines up with Leo Booth's definition of religion as, "a set of man-made principles about God, focusing on a teacher or prophet, in contrast to spirituality, which is the process of becoming a positive and creative person." The Judeo-Christian faiths along with all the other religions of the world all depend on some "ruler" to determine what is good or bad and tell us how we measure up to that standard. But what is that ruler?

Christian groups refer to the Bible as their standard or ruler. But all of them run into the same difficulty of how to interpret the Bible. Generally there are two main methods of interpretation, the literal, historical, grammatical method and the allegorical, figurative method or a combination of both. The first takes the Bible literally while the second views it figuratively. Regardless of the method used, the interpretation of what the Bible actually says can be a long way off from what it really means. It is in the interpretation of the Bible that the Judeo-Christian faiths differ from one another about many issues including the essential nature of man as being good or bad.

> Regardless of the method used, the interpretation of what the Bible actually says can be a long way off from what it really means.

The literal interpretation of the Bible would demand that human nature be viewed as inherently evil due to the original sin of Adam and Eve. This would agree with what Freud said about humanity being essentially evil and the best we could hope for is to return to some acceptable form of dysfunction. The allegorical interpretation of the Bible allows for a different view of human nature as being essentially good. It entertains the possibility that there is nothing inherently evil in human nature. Any references to original sin and the resulting guilt and shame, therefore, are a result of misinterpretations of the Bible. Which one is right? Am I good or bad?

Rather than choose sides and seek to prove one is preferable to the other, we need to consider the possibility that both are wrong and both are right. The literal interpretation of the Bible reveals that we are "born bad". Experience corroborates this view in as much as we do not have to teach small children to be selfish, intolerant, unkind, cruel, ungrateful or insensitive to the needs of others. They are born with a self-centered view of the world and immediately seek to manipulate and control people and things around them in order to satisfy their own needs. Likewise, we may observe the benefits of viewing people, especially children as having tremendous potential for good. Children who are taught early that they are basically a good person capable of caring about others and succeeding in life often behave much better than those who are expected to fail and deserve to be punished. The key to answering the question of am I good or bad, is not in a blanket judgment about human nature based on a literal or figurative interpretation of the Bible, but rather in the understanding of the central theme of the Bible being the good news of all that God has done and continues to do to make us like him (i.e. spiritual enlightenment).

There are two problems that lead to erroneous conclusions.

1. In an attempt to "take the edge off" the personal pain we feel, religious messages and teachings that say we were born bad but can make ourselves good by following the rules of God produce a negative self image in a variety of ways and lead to all forms of addiction.

2. On the other hand, religious messages that say we were born good and, therefore, have the responsibility to act like who we are will simply shift the blame for our addictions and failures away from the individual to the society or environment. The argument is that we are bad, not by virtue of the fact that we were born bad, but by the fact that we are taught that we were born bad. In other words, if we were not taught the concept of original sin and the total depravity of man, then we would not view ourselves as being bad and, therefore, act bad.

Both positions completely miss the real point of the Bible. The Bible does indeed tell us that all are "born bad", but it does not suggest in any way that we can make ourselves good by keeping the rules. In fact, it warns us that such a task is impossible for man to achieve since the ultimate end of all the standards of God is absolute righteousness which demands that we are not born "bad" in the first place. The Bible also recognizes the need to change the way we think of ourselves in order to be healthy and functional. We cannot think of ourselves as being essentially bad and expect to feel or act good. What is the answer then, are we bad or are we good?

The Bible tells us that we are born bad and, therefore, have the need to be born again in order to be good. Being "born again" refers to a radical change in identity that the Bible also describes as being done by God, himself, and not us. It further reveals that God has already done all that is necessary to make us good according to his standards so that all that is necessary for us to do is to believe it. Those who interpret the Bible as a revelation of God's grace in doing for us what we cannot do for ourselves will respond with an authentic faith that is focused on divine provision rather than self effort. Authentic faith will always be expressed in attitudes and actions of tolerance, compassion, and love for others.

Those who interpret the Bible as a book of rules and standards by which we are judged and condemned by God will develop a toxic faith that is focused on self effort rather than divine provision. Toxic faith will express itself in fear, guilt, shame, manipulation, and control of others. It is from the latter interpretation that the various forms of addiction, including religious addiction, are generated. To avoid the pitfalls of addiction we must be able to see ourselves as good, not because we were born that way initially, but because God did all that was necessary to make us good.

Am I Religious Or Spiritual?

Religious addiction is produced when one who is convinced they are worthless (experiencing fear, guilt, shame, and despair) seeks to find a way out of their problems by basing their worth on something other than who God has made them to be. Naturally they turn to religious activities, rituals, dogma, and practices to try to compensate for that deep sense of worthlessness they are experiencing. All too often they find those who are more than happy to provide them with the "rules" they are seeking to make themselves worthy. Their false assumptions may switch from the secular to the sacred. For example, prior to their "conversion" an individual who really believes that they are worthless may try to compensate by becoming wealthy. Their reasoning may be something like, "I will be worthy if I can make more money". After all, how much money we have is a generally accepted indication of our "worth" as a person. People with money are usually viewed as being secure and significant as compared to the poor. But when such a person becomes religious, he will change the basis of his worth from the secular standard of money to the sacred standard of religious performance. He might think, for instance, "I will be worthy if I can meet up to certain performance standards and gain the approval of the authorities in the church or religious group". Although he has changed his false assumptions of personal worth from a secular source to a religious source, the fact is that he still sees himself as being essentially worthless.

Notice how different true spiritual enlightenment is from this sort of religious activity. The person who believes that God has done everything necessary to make them worthy begins to exercise an authentic faith. Rather than saying to themselves, "I will be worthy if ..." they are thinking, "I am worthy because of who God has made me to be". Their faith is in the power of God and not in their own self-effort to perform in a religious way. As a result of their faith in their new identity in God, they now begin to experience a true sense of hope or a joyful and confident expectation about their future. Having their own personal needs met, they are now free to care about the needs of others. They can actually think about someone besides themselves. They can actually love others.

The roots of religious addiction lie in the false assumptions of what it takes to make us worthy as persons. When the statement "I will be worthy if..." is completed with religious activities such as church attendance, Bible reading and study, proselytizing others, giving financially, or trying hard to meet dress codes and certain standards of conduct, the net result will always be religiosity, not true spirituality. Like any other addiction, these religious activities often produce a false sense of satisfaction in much the same way drugs or alcohol can produce a false sense of security and personal significance. Sooner or later, however, the initial "high" wears off and leaves the individual empty again. Being empty inside (or lack of personal worth) drives the religious addict to try even harder to be fulfilled by religious activity and the cycle starts all over again. Doing the same things over and over again expecting different results is characteristic of the insanity known as addiction.

True spiritual enlightenment begins with the recognition that there is a God who can and will do for us what we cannot do for ourselves. It's characterized by a personal, authentic faith that is focused on relationships with God and others rather than on rituals. It is motivated by genuine hope rather than guilt and shame, and expresses itself in compassion for others rather than manipulation or control. In order to be spiritual rather than religious we need only to quit looking at what we are going to do and focus on what God says he has already done for us. Rather than view the Bible as some sort of divine book of rules or directions on how we may save ourselves, we need to view it as a divine revelation of grace and truth necessary to make us healthy.

Summary

The greatest obstacle to developing the skill of spiritual enlightenment is toxic faith producing some form of religious addition. Jesus rebuked the religious leaders of his day for their religiosity which manifested itself in at least three recognizable components. First, he stated that, "they say and do not..." that is, they were able to talk the talk, but not walk the walk. Their hypocrisy was inevitable due to the fact that they were living under the law focusing on their own self efforts rather than trusting the grace of God for their righteousness. Pretending to represent God, they actually rejected his only begotten son. Second, they put heavy burdens on others rather than liberate them. Their perfectionist expectations of and legal demands on others produced only performance-based religion rather than spiritual freedom. Finally, Jesus revealed their true motivation by saying, "all their works they do to be seen of men". Their words and deeds were motivated by seeking the approval of men and full of pride.

> **Jesus' rejection of toxic religious leaders:**
>
> 1. They say and do not.
> 2. They put heavy burden on people.
> 3. All their works they do to be seen of men.

Only the authentic faith that: (1) arises from within the individual, (2) is focused on divine provisions, and (3) expresses itself in tolerance and love for others produces true spirituality. Such spirituality (rather than religion) allows us to be controlled by the Spirit in all that we do or say. We enjoy the privilege of hearing God's voice, following his leadership, receiving his comfort, and experiencing his power in transforming our lives to be more and more like his son. Spirituality, not religiosity, is the key to recovery and a functional healthy life.

Exercises

1. All religions have some elements of toxic faith in them. Take time to review your religious background and identify the toxic faith you may have been exposed to by considering the origin, focus, and expression of your faith.
2. It is common for "baby" believers to fall into some sort of religious activity in seeking to grow spiritually. Describe the ways you may have tried to please God or get God to bless you.
3. The natural toxic faith of the flesh is based upon our "knowledge of good and evil" from which we develop high expectations of us and others. List out seven expectations you have for yourself and seven expectations you have for others. (Note how much higher the expectations for others.)
4. Confess your toxic faith to God and ask him to help you learn all that he has done to make you righteous as a new person in Christ. Write down seven statements God makes in his word, the Bible, to assure you that he has done everything needed in your life to meet his expectations and gain is blessings.

7. Communication skills: The Miracle of Communication

A significant part of relational empowerment is the ability to effectively communicate with others. In relational counseling, one of the most common complaints concerns the lack of appropriate communication. "We can't talk to our child" is a typical parental complaint while "I can't talk to my parents" is typical of adolescents. Likewise, one of the most common complaints among married couples is the lack of any "real" communication. Often the problems associated with communication are not intentional, but due to the lack of basic communication skills.

In the next three chapters we will consider the factors that determine effective communication in our relationships. By understanding the communication process as well as the motivational and content factors that affect it we can develop the communication skills necessary to relate to others in a healthy manner. Real and healthy communication does not happen automatically just because we can talk to each other... it is, in many respects, a miracle. The personal skills discussed in the previous chapters prepare us for developing the communication skills needed to build and maintain relationships. It's now time to begin to exercise those skills in verbal and non-verbal communication.

The Word

In his gospel the Apostle John refers to Jesus as "the Word" signifying that he is absolutely essential to effective communication. He stated, "*In the beginning was the Word and the Word was with God, and the Word was God.*" The literal meaning of the Greek word he uses to describe Jesus as the "Word" is better translated, "discourse", which implies that Jesus is the divine communication of God to mankind. During his life and ministry here on earth Jesus, himself, stated that the words he spoke and the things he did were not his own, but came from the Father. His primary purpose was to communicate all that God wanted to reveal to the world.

The writer of Hebrews describes this divine communication at the outset of his letter by saying, "*In the past God spoke to our forefathers through the prophets at many times and in various ways, but in these last days he has spoken to us by his Son, whom he appointed heir of all things, and through whom he made the universe.*" Note he tells us that Jesus is not simply a way God used to reveal himself to man, but that he is the greatest and final revelation. Jesus is not only a method of communication, but he is also the source of the most effective communication. Apart from his work in our lives through the miraculous working of the indwelling Spirit of God we have no hope for effective communication.

As a practical consideration it is important for us to realize that all effective communication depends on our personal relationship with the "Word." In order to choose the right words to say or decided on the best action to take in communicating with others we must rely upon the personal leadership and power of Jesus through his Spirit living within. Our "vertical" communication with God must precede our "horizontal" communication with others to be effective. Leaving God out of our communication at home, on the job, or in the community is, perhaps, the single biggest cause of our distorted and ineffective communication with others.

This does not mean that we must "talk religion" to have good communication. In fact, religious talk is often a sign of the toxic faith discussed in the last chapter. Including God in our communication is simply a matter of faith. We believe that we can talk to God and hear what he has to say to us. He is the "expert" in all our affairs from finances to employment to housing to recreation as well as our spiritual life. In addition, he knows what we need to communicate to others for their good as well as ours. A failure to consult him makes our communication with others less effective and possibly even destructive.

The good news is that we can rely upon Jesus to empower our communication with others, just as he relied upon the Father to direct him in all that he said or did during his earthly ministry. He is not only willing to speak to others through us as his ambassadors in this world, but has commissioned us to do so. Since his resurrection and ascension back into heaven, the only concrete and tangible expression of Jesus in this world is the Christ others experience through you. This is why Paul describes the church as the "body of Christ". Every believer has the privilege of communicating with God and revealing Christ as a "member of his body". As the frightened little girl said to her daddy to convince him to stay with her in the dark, "We need a Jesus with skin on him!"

The Communication Process

True communication may be described as a four-step process, involving two broad phases... transmission and reception. It begins as one person seeks to express an idea to another, and is completed when that idea is actually perceived as *intended* by the initiator. The first step is to translate the

> **Two Categories of Communication**
> 1. **Transmission**
> 2. **Reception**

thought or idea into appropriate words. At first this may seem simple, but a moment's reflection reveals that we all have trouble accurately expressing our thoughts. Frequently we "say things we didn't mean" especially under pressure. Many times we complain that we "just can't find the right words" to express our thoughts or feelings. Translating our thoughts and ideas into intelligible words is not always easy or automatic. But, it must be done because the responsibility for proper and complete transmission lies with the initiator.

The second step in the communication process involves the medium in which the words are spoken. By medium we are referring to the context and timing of the words we speak. The medium can either enhance or distort the communication. For instance, a wife may want to communicate with her husband about some important family issues during the last quarter of the super bowel game. That medium is not very conducive for real communication and will likely distort or block her efforts to talk. Similarly, a husband may try to talk to his wife while she is at work in the office or home. The medium of a work environment is not always conducive to personal communication and will also tend to completely distort or block it. Again, the responsibility to select the medium is with the initiator.

There are many factors in the medium that would distort the efforts to communicate, but the most important is the "relational noise" referred to in the Bible. "Though I speak with the tongues of men and of angels, and have not love, I am become as sounding brass or a tinkling cymbal" (1 Corinthians 13:1). In other words, I can use the most eloquent words, but if I am not motivated by genuine love for the other, I'm just making noise. That kind of relational noise in the medium distorts or blocks much of our communication.

The third step in the communication process is active listening. Words properly chosen and expressed in an appropriate medium, can only be received if the listener is attentive to what is being said. All too often the communication process breaks down at this point due to the fact that the listener is too busy trying to think up a response to pay attention to what is actually being said. Active listening is necessary to insure effective communication. It involves an effort on the part of the listener to make sure he has really heard the words spoken. The importance of this step in communication may be illustrated by the fact that we are created with two ears and only one mouth. This implies we need to listen twice as much as we speak. Later we will consider some techniques to improve our ability to listen, but for now it is sufficient to know that this step is vital for effective communication.

The last step in the communication process is that of interpretation. When the words spoken are accurately heard, they must be interpreted in the mind of the listener to arrive at the true meaning of the original thought expressed. Once again the communication process can be blocked if the words heard are not accurately interpreted. Hearing words and understanding the meaning of those words is not the same thing. Often we have a tendency to "read more into the words" than was originally intended by the speaker. This is especially true under stressful conditions such as arguments and fights in the family. Given a history of strife in a relationship, it is not unusual for the listener to assume, based upon "history'" that the speaker "doesn't really mean" what was just said and interpret his words in some other way. The listener must seek clarification rather than assuming something that was not intended. True communication only occurs when the idea or thought in the mind of the speaker is accurately reproduced in the mind of the listener.

We have two fundamental and obvious requirements for true communication. In the transmission phase we must have accurate and meaningful expression at the right time, in the right place. Second, in the reception phase, we must be actively and accurately tuned in and ready to receive. The potential in any of these four steps, in either phase, to distort or block communication is so great that it truly is a miracle when two people actually communicate.

Exercising the personal skills discussed in previous chapters sets the stage for the miracle of communication to occur. To the extent we are willing and able to practice cognitive restructuring, emotional management, behavioral redirection, and spiritual enlightenment, these steps of communication can be understood and practiced so that we may develop healthy communication skills. Although it may appear to be a very complicated process, it really is much simpler in actual practice. Describing the process of communication is much more complicated than actually communicating. When people really want to communicate, persistent efforts to learn the skills necessary will be rewarded with improved communication.

The Miracle of Communication

As mentioned earlier, there is a very real miraculous component to effective communication... not only because there are so many ways for it to break down, but also because the Bible makes it clear that effective communication requires divine intervention. James 3 warns, *"And the tongue is a fire, a world of iniquity: so is the tongue among our members, that it defileth the whole body, and setteth on fire the course of nature; and it is set on fire of hell...But the tongue can no man tame; it is an unruly evil, full of deadly poison"*.

> **James 3**
>
> *"And the tongue is a fire, a world of iniquity: so is the tongue among our members, that it defileth the whole body, and setteth on fire the course of nature; and it is set on fire of hell...But the tongue can no man tame; it is an unruly evil, full of deadly poison"*

Ever since the Tower of Babel incident in which God "confounded their language" we have had trouble achieving effective communication and needed to depend on divine provisions to overcome our weakness.

In both the talking and the listening side of communication the miracle occurs through the personal work of the Holy Spirit in our lives. Simply put, we rely upon the Spirit to give us the wisdom and words for effective communication with others and the ability to hear and understand what others are saying. This double–edged miracle may best be illustrated by the miraculous gift of "tongues" on the day of Pentecost referred to in Acts 2. Beginning with Peter, the apostles gave witness to the resurrection of Christ in their own native language, yet Jews from all over the world heard what they were saying in their own native tongue. Clearly, the miracle of effective communication there was a miracle of hearing in those who were listening to the apostle's message.

In assuring his disciples in their role as witnesses for him, Jesus told them not to worry about what they were going to say ahead of time...he promised them the right words would be given them just when they needed it. A significant part of the spiritual enlightenment we receive involves the personal leadership of the Spirit in how we communicate with others. As Paul reminds us in 1 Corinthians 13, our most eloquent speech is nothing more than just making noise if it is not motivated by divine love. However, words motivated by the love of the Spirit and spoken in the leadership and power of the Spirit are essential for effective communication. It is the miraculous power of the indwelling Spirit that makes the difference.

Summary

A primary part of relational empowerment involves effective communication skills. In order for us to actually love others like Christ we have to be skilled in communicating both verbally and non-verbally. Like the personal skills studied earlier, communication skills are not automatic in our natural condition. Although we are capable of talking and acting in our relationships, all such verbal and non-verbal behavior on a natural level is still self centered unless it is motivated by the miraculous work of the Holy Spirit living within us. Naturally, we can't find the right words to say or think of the appropriate things to do to love others like Christ because we are too busy thinking about ourselves.

The miracle of effective and accurate communication occurs when we allow ourselves to be controlled by the Spirit of God and follow his leadership in our relationships. Our selfishness is replaced by the love we need to properly motivate our words and actions (i.e. the "fruit of the Spirit"). Confusion about what to say or do is miraculously cleared up when we trust the Spirit to guide us into all truth and lead us to love others. One of the greatest privileges we have as children of God is to be used of him to effectively communicate his love to those around us.

Exercises

1. Review the communication process by writing across a sheet of paper the words: translation, medium, listening, and interpretation. Underneath each of these words give an example from your own experience that demonstrates the problems we may encounter in trying to communicate with others.

2. The following complaints demonstrate communication difficulties:
   a. "I didn't mean to say that"
   b. "I thought you said..."
   c. "I didn't hear you say..."
   d. "This is not a good time to talk"
   e. "I can never think of anything to say"
   f. "You are always telling me..."
   g. "You are too busy to talk"

   Next to each of the above statements write the component of the communication process that best describes the problem area.

3. The miracle of effective communication is accomplished by the leadership and power of the indwelling Spirit of God. Ask God to remind you daily that communication is a miracle from him and start communicating through prayer and meditation with him personally.

8. Communication skills: Speaking the Truth in Love

Ministry or Manipulation?

Like all other behavior communication may be motivated by faith, hope, and love; or it can be motivated by fear, guilt, or pride. Effective communication is motivated by love rather than pride, hope rather than guilt, and faith rather than fear. In short, effective communication ministers grace to the hearer. As we have discussed earlier, the natural motivations of our flesh continually block effective communication due to the lack of divine love. The words chosen or the topics discussed may be the same, but the motivation behind them makes all the difference in how the communication is transmitted and how it is received. Words motivated by selfishness, defensiveness, or boastfulness, will block rather than enhance communication.

In Ephesians 4 Paul warns us about the natural communication of the flesh by saying, *"Let no corrupt communication proceed out of your mouth, but that which is good to the use of edifying, that it may minister grace to the hearers."* The typical religious interpretation of this warning usually defines corrupt communication as some sort of profanity or vulgar speech. However, the literal meaning of corrupt communication" is far more than using four-letter words or slang…it is speaking words that tear down or hurt another. Anything we say or do that hurts another or runs them down is considered to be "corrupt communication".

Earlier in the same context of Ephesians 4 Paul admonishes us to, "put away lying". The natural inclination of the flesh with its carnal mind is to lie to ourselves and others. This is especially true when we consider the most fundamental lies we speak to ourselves and others concern our worth as persons. The typical lies of our self talk in the, "I will be worthy if…" format plagues every one of us

103

from birth. Due to our natural failure to believe the truth about our true identity in Christ making us secure in God's love and significant in his plan, we are filled with lies about our own worth being contingent upon our performance, the approval of others, or our circumstances. These same lies spill over into our beliefs about the worth of others as well.

We have a natural tendency to evaluate the worth of others in the same way we do ourselves and typically confuse their behavior or circumstances with their identity. For instance, if I tend to base my worth as a person on my own performance I am apt to do the same for you. I will be thinking, "you will be worthy if you meet up to certain standards". Although I might be hopeful that you will meet that standard, right now I consider you to be somewhat worthless and may even judge you to be unlovable and deserving some sort of punishment. Any verbal or non-verbal communication I might initiate toward you will be tainted by my own false assumption about your worth as a person. I may even use encouraging words, but the motivation behind those words (never mind the non-verbal cues such as tone of voice or facial expressions) is likely to be that of manipulation rather than ministry.

Believing that you are now worthless, but you will be worthy if you meet my standards, I am also likely to identify you with your poor performance. I may identify you as a failure because you failed, a quitter because you quit, or whiner because you cried when I tried to talk to you! Confusing your behavior with your identity reinforces the lie that you are worthless unless you perform and will usually put an end to any real or effective communication. This is why Paul insists that we quit lying and learn to speak the truth in love.

Paul goes on to tell us how we are going to quit lying by speaking the truth to others. Like all other issues of the Christian life in grace, we cannot simply move into some sort of neutral zone where we are not lying, but we are not speaking the truth either. Such a zone does not exist. We are either going to speak the truth or lie every time we open our mouth to communicate with others. The key to not lying, then, is to speak the truth. Likewise he goes on to tell us how we are going to keep all corrupt communication from coming out of our mouth...by speaking, "that which is good to the use of edifying, that it may minister grace to the hearers." Rather than make statements that hurt and tear down others, we must learn to speak the truth that will build them up and minister grace to them. Reminding ourselves and others of our worth in Christ as we seek to communicate is not a religious "add on", but absolutely vital to effective communication.

Life Words or Death Words?

Applying the personal skills we've studied is critical if we want to improve our communication with others. There is no way to speak the truth in love if we don't know the truth and don't have the divine love we need. The main goal of the personal skills is not just our own comfort, but the preparation we need to be able to communicate effectively with others. As stated before, only those words motivated by divine love can be welcomed and received by the listener. This is especially true in times of misunderstanding or conflict within our relationships. Words spoken to manipulate others are selfish in nature and may be referred to as "death" words because they destroy relationships. They stifle and retard true communication. Those spoken to build up and minister grace to others are selfless in nature and may be referred to as "life" words. Only words motivated by divine love will be truly received by others, even when they are not pleasing to the listener.

For example, parental instruction motivated by genuine love is not only vital to the development of children, but also necessary for the child's immediate sense of personal worth. No matter what words are spoken to convey that instruction, the motivation of love impacts the child's need for personal security and significance. On the other hand, those words motivated by manipulative pride will result in a rebellious attitude regardless of how true they may be at the time. Such "death" words occur when we fail to consider person-al needs of love and respect in the one with whom we are trying to communi-cate. Death words are selfish, life words are selfless. The Bible warns parents to avoid such communication when it says, *"And ye fathers, provoke not your children to wrath..."* (Ephesians 6:4). Communication motivated by pride rather than love will always provoke the hearer to wrath, whether children or adults.

> **Ephesians 6:4**
>
> Ye fathers, provoke not your children to wrath...

In order to insure that our words are properly motivated by love, it is necessary to consider the other two motivational factors that underlie them. To avoid the selfishness and manipulative pride that is so natural in our communication, we must first be assured that our own needs are met. This requires an exercise of faith in choosing to believe that we are worthy as persons (secure and significant) regardless of the behavior of others. Such faith will produce a sense of hope (joyful confidence) in our own future that frees us to actually care about the welfare of others more than our own. Practicing the personal skills described in the previous chapters is the personal preparation we need to exercise that faith and experi-ence that hope necessary to actually speak life words rather than death words. Only "life words" will produce effective communica-tion; "death words" will distort or destroy communication altogeth-er.

Time Out for the Trip In

Before seeking to communicate with others, especially family mem-bers, it is useful to communicate with God, not just to seek advice but also to seek insight into our own inward motivations. This is what is meant by the "trip in". It is really just evaluating our underlying beliefs, emotions, and motivations before we try to communicate to others. It is here that the personal skills are essential. Being able to hear God's voice and receive divine assurance concerning our own needs and direction in our day to day interchange with others is the best preparation for speaking the truth in love.

As important as it is, however, taking the time to communicate with the Father is not natural to our everyday experience. Typically we try to communicate with others based on our own "knowledge of good and evil" or our own understanding of what is right and what is wrong. Even though we may prove what we think is right or wrong using our understanding of the Bible; the "truth" we are trying to communicate is never really heard because it is not spoken in love. Remember, without being motivated by divine love our most eloquent speech is "just making noise" no matter how true it may be. Hence, we desperately need to communicate with God before we try to communicate with others. Such quick and personal prayers are very helpful in developing and maintaining our own sense of worth as well as reinforcing our knowledge of the truth.

Although prayers of this nature are an invaluable resource of personal strength, they are often overlooked in the "heat of the battle". It is for this reason that a "time out for the trip in" policy should be established and followed. Any time our communication degenerates into an argument, no one really wins. Arguments can easily escalate into verbal abuse or violence that will be regretted later. As the negative emotions begin to rise up in us its time to take a time out in order to utilize our personal skills. A failure to do so will allow the negative feelings to degenerate quickly into destructive and sinful emotions. A few moments alone with the Lord can do much to restore a sense of personal worth and the motivation of love. As the emotional turmoil subsides, it is more likely that real and meaningful communication may occur.

Taking time out to do the trip in is simply an honest evaluation of our own situation, words, feelings, and beliefs. It is a time of personal reflection in which we stop to consider ourselves, not those we are fighting with. During this trip in we will discover our own false assumptions, destructive emotions, death words, and attempts to manipulate others. While this may be somewhat painful at first, it should not be avoided. It is in this time that we are able to rid ourselves of the false assumptions, sinful emotions, and prideful behavior by simply confessing it to God and allowing him to forgive us (send it away) and cleanse us. When we take time to reaffirm our true identity in Christ and make the distinction between who we are and our ever present flesh; we are actually "walking in the light as he is in the light". The result is that we have fellowship with God and the blood of Jesus Christ will keep on cleansing us from all sin. In essence, then, the trip in is a personal cleansing and preparation for us to be able to effectively communicate with others, even those we argue with.

It is important to note that the "trip in" need not last for hours or days, but may actually be done in a matter of minutes. The spiritual enlightenment that results from our communication with God often changes our perceptions, cools heated emotions, and tempers our responses in seconds. This miraculous work of the indwelling Spirit of God does not take long and can be done repeatedly. Taking time to do the trip in can even be done in the midst of a conversation. Consider the injunction of Paul for us to "pray without ceasing". All too often we get the idea that we cannot talk to some one else and talk to God at the same time. This difficulty usually stems from the idea that prayer is "polite speech" to God. But actually, prayer is at least as much hearing from God as it is talking to him; and you are quite capable of hearing him while engaged in a conversation with another. In that sense you are "praying without ceasing" even in your conversations with others.

Because the purpose of the trip in is divine cleansing and prepa-ration for ministry, the real work is done by the indwelling Spirit, not by any rituals we might devise. Therefore, the trip in is better described as awareness of our need and a willingness on our part to allow God to replace the thoughts, feelings, and words of the flesh with those of the Spirit. Such a dependency on the Spirit is referred to by Paul as, "walking in the Spirit". The trip in, then, is simply a descriptive term for allowing the Spirit to expose and eliminate the selfish tendencies of the flesh, and replace them with the character of Christ. The overall result of the trip in is that Christ is living his life through us and communicating with others through us... as us!

Changing from the Inside Out

During the trip in we are allowing God to change us from the inside out by the renewing of our mind, comforting us emotionally, and redirecting our behavior. In a sense, God is in the process of giving us a spiritual "make over" to conform us to the image of his son, Jesus. The net result is that we are able to speak his life words with power and all the authority of heaven! We are ambassadors for Christ in our communication with others and, therefore, need to be continuously changed from the inside out to be effective.

Because we yet possess the leftovers of who we used to be as a natural descendant of Adam, what the Bible calls the flesh, we are often plagued with the mind of the flesh known as the "carnal" or natural mind. Communication that is done with the carnal mind will always be self-centered at best and manipulative at worst. In order to speak the truth to others we must learn to "put off the old man, be renewed in the Spirit of our mind, and put on the new man". This inward change in our belief systems will also effect changes in our emotions and motives, allowing us to experience the hope we need to actually be concerned about others.

The same change is called for in connection with presenting our bodies as living sacrifices unto God in Romans 12:1, 2. We are commanded to, *"be not conformed to this world, but to be trans-formed by the renewing of our minds"*. This miraculous renewing of the mind we have discussed earlier in connection with the person-al skill of spiritual enlightenment. Essentially it is the work of the

Comforter in changing our false assumptions to Biblical assumptions of personal worth, preventing our negative emotions from decomposing into sinful destructive emotions, and leading us to say the things that are necessary to love others. His part is power, our part is faith. We simply trust the Spirit to do the work he promised to do to change us into the image of Christ.

The "renewing of the mind" is a biblical term for no longer using our natural, carnal mind in favor of learning to use the mind of Christ. At first it may not seem like it, but all believers have the mind of Christ as a significant part of the new person God has made us to be. Even the most carnal Christians in the New Testament, the Corinthians, were told by Paul that they had the mind of Christ. The problem is not whether or not we have the mind of Christ, but whether or not we will use it. All of us have a lot of things we never use. Our garages and closets are filled with them. That's why Paul commanded the Philippians to, *"Let this mind be in you which was also in Christ Jesus."* (Philippians 2:5)

A quick review of the difference between the characteristics of the carnal mind and the mind of Christ reveals what changes we might see in ourselves as the Spirit renews our minds. To begin with, the Spirit will convince us of our true identity as the children of God. The first and greatest characteristic of the mind of Christ was that he knew who he was. When he was twelve years old Jesus recognized that God was his real Father and that he needed to be about his business. Likewise, when we realize that God is our real Father we can let our earthly dads off the hook and quit blaming them for all our troubles.

Secondly, the mind of Christ was willing to give up his rights or, literally, "made himself of no reputation". Knowing who you are is not a reason for insisting that other people minister to you or, at least, appreciate and care about you. The mind of Christ is willing to let all human recognition and approval go because it cannot compare with the acceptance of the Father.

Third, the mind of Christ takes on the form of a servant. Jesus realized his mission was to serve others rather than to be served by others. Because he knew who he was, he was willing to take upon himself the form of a servant to others. Notice how different this mind is from the carnal mind that continually jockeys for position to manipulate and control others.

Fourth, Jesus was willing to identify himself with others, rather than simply compare himself to them or seek to make himself look good at their expense. The carnal mind is continuously engaged in a comparison process. Naturally we seek to define ourselves through a variety of never ending comparisons and contrasts. Of course, we will always find those who seem to be better than we are, but that finding is quickly mitigated as we find those who are worse. Rather than judge others, Jesus identified himself with all of humanity…good, bad, and ugly. At his baptism he explained to the reluctant prophet that he must be baptized along with those who were confessing their sin and dysfunction in order to "fulfill righteousness". By this he meant that he must identify himself with the most vile and filthy sinner in order for that sinner to be able to identify himself with the righteousness of Christ.

Fifth, the mind of Christ is one of genuine humility. He did not think of himself as being less than others, but thought of himself less than he thought of others. True humility is not an exercise in self abasement…that's false humility. Genuine humility is actually the freedom to become more concerned with the welfare of others than you are of your own. This characteristic of the mind of Christ is absolutely vital to "active listening". In order to effectively communicate with others we must be able to care about them more than we care about ourselves.

Sixth, the mind of Christ is completely submissive and obedient to the will of the Father regardless of the cost. He maintained his obedience even unto the shameful death of the cross. A willingness to yield ourselves to the will of God despite what consequences we may suffer is radically different from the attitude of the carnal mind.

Naturally we are continually asking ourselves, "What's in it for me?" expressing our concern for how we will be affected. Being self-centered the carnal mind cannot possibly submit to the Father's will, but insists on its own will.

Finally, the mind of Christ experiences the exaltation and glory

THE MIND OF CHRIST
1. Knows who he or she is.
2. Is willing to give up his rights.
3. Takes on the form of a servant.
4. Identifies with all of humanity... good, bad, and ugly.
5. Is genuinely humble.
6. Is completely submissive to the will of his Father.
7. Experiences the exaltation and glory of God.

of God raising us up to a higher position than we were in before. After the crucifixion came the exaltation...the "joy that was set before him"...that gave Jesus the endurance to suffer the cross. The carnal mind cannot perceive this exaltation and glory that satisfies our deepest needs. It is so bound to the temporary pleasures of this world that such eternal satisfaction is not even a consideration.

It is this personal and spiritual transformation in our minds that prepares us for effective communication. Only when we can think, feel, and talk like Jesus are we ready to communicate the love of God to others at home, on the job, or in the community around us. The good news is that God is already in the process of changing us from the inside out so that we may speak the truth in love and minister grace in our communication.

Summary

Speaking the truth in love is a biblical description of effective communication. In order to love others like
Christ we must develop this communication skill to such an extent that

> Speaking the truth in love is a biblical description of effective communication.

it becomes second nature to us. There are two aspects to this skill
that help us remember what it involves in our daily lives. First, we
are going to speak the truth...not lies. This means that we are going
to have to know the truth ourselves and be able to share it with
others. Jesus called the Comforter the Spirit of Truth and promised
that he would not only be among us, but in us as well. It is the
indwelling Spirit of God that "guides us into all truth" as he renews
our minds on a daily basis. Knowing the truth about ourselves is
absolutely essential to satisfy our own needs for love and respect.
When these needs are satisfied we are free to concern ourselves with
the welfare of others around us. In a sense, we need to speak the
truth to ourselves before we can speak the truth to others.

The second aspect concerns the motivation behind the words
and actions we use to communicate with others. Only that which is
motivated by divine love will be effective. Regardless of how much
truth we may know or seek to communicate, without love it is
perceived only as "noise" and will irritate and frustrate the listener.

> TWO ASPECTS OF SPEAKING THE TRUTH IN
> LOVE
> 1. Speak the truth. Know the truth about
>   ourselves and share it.
> 2. Only that motivated by divine love will be
>   effective.

As the indwelling Spirit renews our minds we receive the love that only comes from God himself. This love is divine in nature and is a substantial part of the miracle of communication. Because it is God's character, divine love is unconditional rather than conditional, sacrificial rather than convenient, initiating rather than reactive, eternal rather than temporary, and intelligent rather than romantic. As the Spirit renews our minds he fills us with the love of God needed to speak the truth in love.

Exercises

1. Give several examples from your own experience that illustrate the difference between "death words" and "life words". Site the difference in terms of what things you have said to others and what you have heard others say to you. Notice the feelings associated with speaking and hearing death words and speaking and hearing life words.

2. Review a recent argument you had with another in terms of the trip in. Describe the situation you were in, the things you said or did, the emotions you were feeling and the thoughts about yourself you were having. Although it may be awkward at first, practicing such introspection will become easier and more automatic in time.

3. Doing the trip in we become aware of our own destructive behaviors, emotions, and false assumptions. Such awareness, however, is not sufficient to change us…it merely points out the need for change. The personal work of the Holy Spirit in renewing our minds will be needed. Having identified you own false assumptions, ask God to renew your mind to believe the truth about your own security and significance.

4. Notice that simply choosing to believe the truth that we are secure and significant does little to change our emotions. Genuine faith includes action on our part. We must also choose to act responsibly by seeking to minister. Review

the situations listed above and describe what you think God would have you do or say to minister to the needs of others. The choice here is simply between proving yourself right so you can "win" the argument, or being used of God to minister to the other's personal need. Your choice to minister despite the argument and your own hurt feelings is what genuine faith looks like.

9. Communication skills: What to Talk About

Having considered the motivational factors of our communication we turn our attention to the content. What do parents say to their children to raise them correctly? What do couples talk about when they spend quality time together? What are we going to share with our friends and acquaintances? The content of our communication is often just as important as the motivation. What is said can

> The content of our communication is often just as important as the motivation.

have as much impact on the listener as why it was said.

Family members often complain that their communication is too superficial. "All we ever talk about is the weather...we never discuss the important things." But what are those "important things"? How do we determine what are superficial issues and what are core issues? What may be an earth-shattering subject for an adolescent is probably considered superficial to adults. Likewise, what may be considered important to a husband is often viewed as frivolous to their wives. How do we determine what is a superficial issue and what is a core issue for all people?

Core Issues

Core issues are those having to do with a person's basic identity, self-worth, and needs. While asking a group of parents to make a list of issues they should talk to their kids about, I was mildly shocked to note that they knew they should talk to their kids about school, their friends, drugs and alcohol, and a host of other issues. But no one suggested that we should talk to our kids about their own identities, their personal needs, or the ways they believed that they could satisfy those needs. Regardless of how important the other

117

issues may be, compared to the core issues of a healthy identity and a genuine sense of personal worth, such issues are superficial. In fact, these other issues hinge on personal identification, self worth and personal needs.

Many parents have made the mistake of talking to their kids about school activities, household chores, and becoming responsible adults without considering their child's personal needs or affirming their personal worth. "Preaching" about the dangers of sex, drugs, and rock n' roll without explaining how false assumptions of personal worth determine both behavior and feelings puts the "cart before the horse" and has a tendency to frustrate rather than encourage our kids.

Similarly, husbands are often guilty of communicating with their wives on a "logical" level rather than considering her need for security (love, acceptance, and forgiveness). Proving that our opinion is "right" by the rules of logic completely misses the core issue of our spouse's personal needs and true identity. It is possible to be absolutely "right" and relationally dead at the same time. Wives also fall prey to the temptation of "nagging" their husbands into agreement rather than communicating while understanding his basic need for significance (importance, meaning, and adequacy). Without addressing the basic personal needs and the assumptions we have concerning how those needs are met, it is impossible to experience anything but superficial communication. This is not to say that there is no overlap in both genders with security and adequacy needs... there is. Men, as well as women, seek and need security (love, acceptance, and forgiveness). Women, as well as men, seek and need significance (importance, meaning, and adequacy). But each gender approaches these differently.

Meaningful communication in the family and elsewhere must include the core as well as the superficial issues. However, communication about the superficial issues must hinge upon a proper understanding of the core issues. Even though it is not "natural" to discuss our personal needs and how they are met through the divine provisions of God, effective communication demands that we learn to dig beneath the superficial issues to recognize and discuss the core issues. The biblical injunction given to fathers not to "provoke their children to wrath" is followed by the command to "bring them up in the nurture and admonition of the Lord." Talking only about the superficial issues is the primary way fathers "provoke" their children or exasperate them. What children really need

"Do not Provoke their children to wrath."

and

"Bring them up in the nurture and admonition of the Lord."

cannot be given by a lecture on what is right or wrong concerning various issues. To bring them up in the "nurture" (security and love) and the "admonition" (significance and respect) of the Lord means that we teach them to rely upon divine provisions to satisfy their personal needs. Such instruction requires talking about the core issues as well as the superficial.

Questions such as, "How are you feeling about yourself?" or, "what do you think about yourself? Begin to probe beneath the surface and explore the core issues. While it is important to listen carefully to the superficial issues being discussed, effective communication goes beyond to discuss the underlying personal issues of identity and personal needs. Listening to people vent their feelings of frustration due to certain circumstances is useful, but the assurance and comfort they really need to deal with that frustration will only come from addressing the underlying core issues. Discussing what is right and what is wrong may offer some temporary relief for those who are struggling with superficial issues, but only dis-

Discussing what is right and what is wrong may offer some temporary relief for those who are struggling with superficial issues, but only discussing core issues involving the truth of our worth in Christ will satisfy their deepest needs.

cussing core issues involving the truth of our worth in Christ will satisfy their deepest needs.

Letting God Talk

Addressing the core issues of personal identity and worth is neither natural nor easy at first. Being able to look beneath the surface of the superficial issues and discuss the personal core issues requires a basic understanding of the gospel for one's self as well as others. We must begin with belief in the fact that we are, in fact, already secure in God's love and significant in his plan regardless of how threatening the superficial issues may look. This requires an unshakable faith in the gospel of grace. Believing that others are worthy despite their worthless behavior often takes mountain moving faith! Communication on this level means we are going to trust God to do most of the talking to us and to others. We are going to need the comfort and assurance that only he can provide to enter into a dialogue about core issues.

A word of caution may be useful here. Many people are reluctant and uncomfortable in talking about core issues. They prefer to stay on a superficial level because of the personal pain they are experiencing. Effective communication does not mean that we force people to talk about their own core issues. They can be encouraged when we are simply willing to discuss the core issues, especially when we are able to empathize with them by putting ourselves in their situation. Sometimes talking about our own struggle rather than theirs is enough to give them the courage to at least think about their core issues. When their real pain and frustration is coming from their beliefs about their own identity and worth as opposed to the superficial issues they complain about, it's going to take more than our words to help. Ultimately they need to hear from God. The best we can do for them is to share our own struggle in this area as an example of how believing the gospel gives us relief.

Knowing when to talk is just as important as knowing what to talk about. Long periods of silence, especially when talking about painful core issues, are common and should not be avoided by quickly changing the subject back to superficial issues. A good rule of thumb to follow comes from the realization that we have two ears, but only one mouth. Generally, it is wise to listen twice as much as you speak for effective communication to take place. Remember, you can hear God directing you while listening to someone else talk; and those we are communicating with also need time to process what is being said. God seems to speak the loudest during those awkward periods of silence. Don't interrupt him by continually talking to relieve the strain. When you do speak, keep the 30 second rule in mind…after 30 seconds of talking you are no longer communicating, but are now preaching.

> Knowing when to talk is just as important as knowing what to talk about.

Yet another important communication skill involves learning to accept rather than reject other people's emotions. Feelings are among the most personal things we can talk about. Those who share their true feelings run the risk of not only having their feelings rejected, but also being rejected as a person simply because they have those feelings.

> Feelings are among the most personal things we can talk about.

This is especially true of longstanding or chronic feelings of hatred, despair, or anxiety. In seeking to talk about core issues we will invariably encounter strong emotions. How we handle those emotions determines the quality of our communication.

The personal skill of emotional management is vital to our ability to communicate with others. Being honest with God about our feelings and allowing him to affirm us personally prepares us to minister to others by accepting rather than rejecting their feelings. All too often we treat other people's feelings like a bag full of stinky garbage...we do or say anything just to get rid of them. Some typical ways to reject the feelings of others are a quick apology, a strong reprimand, or immediate advice. The goal of each of these responses is to eliminate the feelings thereby rejecting them. In contrast, acceptance of another's feelings will involve repeating them, exploring them, and describing them. Here the goal is not to quickly dispose of them, but to experience them... "to weep with those who weep and rejoice with those who rejoice". How we handle other people's feelings ultimately earns us the right to remind them of the truth in that it demonstrates our love for them. People are open to receiving anything you have to say if they are sure you love them.

Actions Speak Louder Than Words

There are no words that can communicate as effectively as our own example. The old saying, "actions speak louder than words," reveals the most effective way to communicate to our family members and others. This is especially true when dealing with children. We learn to live life by a process called "modeling." This simply means that we all, young and old, learn by watching others, and trying to "model" their behavior. For our words to have a real impact on others, they not only need to address the core as well as superficial issues, but also be consistent with our behavior. Simply instructing others to, "do what I say and not as I do", is not sufficient to prevent the modeling of harmful or unwanted behaviors. "Walking the walk" rather than simply "talking the talk" is the most efficient way to communicate in our relationships. Words can only have real meaning when they are supported by actions.

When a parent finally gives into the manipulative whining of a child, their reluctant permission is usually attended by non-verbal cues such as facial expressions or tone of voice that communicate their frustration. Their words may say yes," but their behavior is saying "no." Such double-bind messages create confusion at best and frustration at worst. Likewise, a wife who tells her husband that she loves him and wants to stay married, but continues flirting with other men and engaging in extra-marital affairs; not only creates confusion within the family, but also destroys all relationships. The hypocrisy of saying one thing with our words and another with our actions undermines any real communication.

Double-bind messages are damaging to our relationships in that they block effective communication. They come from the uncertainty we have due to relying upon our own knowledge of good and evil rather than the personal leadership of the Spirit. We might believe that what we say is technically correct, but we don't feel comfortable with the decision. "I think this is what you ought to do according to what I know is right and wrong, but I feel very uncomfortable about it." Such ambivalent messages are clearly not from God, but from our own insecure flesh and may be just as harmful to the relationship as negative messages. It is far better to let God decide what is best and allow him to talk to us through his Spirit.

The Blessing

When considering what to talk about in our communication, nothing is more important than to understand the power of the gospel in the lives of others. Paul tells us he was not ashamed of (was willing to talk about) the gospel of Jesus Christ and explains that it is the power of God unto salvation to all who will believe! The good news of the gospel is the most important thing we can communicate to our family, friends, and the world! Whatever else we may discuss, the gospel of grace needs to be part of the dialogue in some fashion to fully develop our communication skills.

This does not mean that we become religious in our communication. One of the early church fathers put it this way, "Witness every day for Christ…and if you must, use words." The idea here is our conversations do not need to be religious in nature to be centered in the gospel of grace. As a matter of fact, it is quite possible for us to believe the gospel for others (i.e. that they are worthy) and not quote the Bible or use the words Jesus or God in our conversation with them. When we believe the gospel ourselves, we experience the love we need to demonstrate that we are followers of Christ without having to announce it formally in our conversations. Remember, one of the most subtle traps of the enemy is to cover our true spirituality with religiosity. Since the ultimate goal of our conversations with others is to tell them they are worthy rather than prove our own worth, it is not necessary to use religious language to love and respect them.

The most useful communication skill we may develop is that of blessing others with the gospel of grace. All people are, by nature, personally insecure and insignificant in their natural condition. Every day their soul hungers for security and thirsts for significance. While we cannot meet these needs in them (only a relationship to Christ can satisfy them) we can be used by God to make them feel their worth by the words we speak and the things we do. Loving, accepting, and forgiving them by words and deeds will make them feel secure. Respecting, encouraging, and supporting them will make them feel significant. In short, believing the gospel for them, that is, believing that God has made them worthy as persons, will go a long way towards helping them to believe it for themselves.

Nowhere is this skill more needed than in the family. In their book, *The Blessing*, (1986, Nelson Publishers) Gary Smalley and John Trent outline five important elements of the family blessing. It should include:

- Meaningful, appropriate touch
- A spoken message of hope
- Attaching "high value" to the one being blessed
- Picturing a special future for the one being blessed
- An active commitment to fulfill the blessing

Learning to communicate family "blessings" rather than with-holding them or, worse yet, communicating family "curses", is one of the most valuable tools we can use to build our relationships. Each family member desperately needs to have their personal needs for security and significance met in a concrete and tangible way. The blessing helps each member of the family feel the reality of their own personal worth.

While it is true that only God can truly satisfy our needs for worth, He has chosen to use us to make others feel worthy. Even though God establishes our worth, and satisfies our need for worth, he uses people to make people feel worthy. This is the basic purpose of personal relationships. To tell family members they are worthy because of what God has made them to be in Christ is well and good. But to make them feel the reality of their worth by the blessing is the more excellent way of love.

In seeking the opportunity to bless others we will naturally become more positive in our communication. Rather than wait for others to make a mistake and jump on them about it, we will be trying to "catch them doing something right" so that we may praise them. As always our goal is to minister the love of Christ to our family members. Communicating the blessing will go far toward reaching this goal.

Summary

What we talk about in our every day conversations has a major impact on our relationships. In fact, Jesus said it's not what goes into the mouth that defiles a man, but what comes out, "For out of the abundance of the heart, the mouth speaks". We have already seen how damaging our own self-talk can be to our emotions. Likewise, "corrupt communication" destroys our relationships to others. Healthy communication skills allow us to talk with others about the core issues of personal worth relying on the Sprit of Truth to guide and empower our words.

For our communication to be healthy for us and edifying to others we must also be skilled in blessing those we talk with. This blessing is not to be confused with "religious talk", or "preaching", but occurs when we truly believe in and affirm the gospel of grace as it applies not only to us, but also to others. We simply choose to believe that those we are speaking to are just as worthy as we are despite the evidence to the contrary; that faith in the gospel allows us to communicate love and respect for others in all that we say and do. When we become skilled in communicating the "life words" of the gospel to others around us, it not only edifies them, but also reinforces our own sense of personal worth.

Exercises

1. List seven important issues or topics you would like to talk about with people in your life at home, on the job, or in the community. Now compare those issues to the definition of "core issues" and note how many of our important issues in life are really superficial rather than core issues.

2. In contrasting superficial with core issues we are not suggesting that they are not important things to talk about. How you spend your time, energy, and money, for example, are all important things to consider and talk about. How your kids behave at home and in school; what's going on at work; how your family and friends behave are equally important issues that need to be discussed. However, the underlying issues of personal needs and how they are or are not being met in every situation are the core issues that motivate all that we do or say. Review your list of issues and redefine them in terms of personal needs for your self and each person concerned.

3. Next to each of the issues you listed write down what you think God is saying to you about your own personal needs being met as well as the needs of the others involved. Note that the comfort you receive from God meeting your needs will begin to prepare you to minister to the needs of the others involved in each situation.

4. Write out another list of personal needs that all people have to have met every day to live and function in a healthy way. Assuming that you believe the good news that God is meeting your needs, write out what statements you might make to others about their needs for worth. Remember, it's not just your words that they will hear, but your attitude and motivation for those words.

5. For each of the people involved in your list begin to formulate a blessing for them. Applying the gospel of grace to them, write down what things you believe God might want you to share with them about their personal worth and how that relates to the superficial issues you originally wanted to talk about with them. Notice that your communication with them is much deeper than the original topic and will likely be more interesting than just the superficial issue itself.

10. Relational Ministry

Thus far in our study we have considered the things that are necessary to prepare us to love others. The personal and communication skills are the skills needed to be able to develop and maintain healthy relationships at any level of intimacy. They are foundational in the sense that without them our relationships will be devoid of the divine love we are called to give to one another. We cannot give what we do not have. It is impossible to love others like Jesus without having his love to share. The personal and communication skills we have outlined in the previous chapters describe how we can receive the love we need to give others.

Now we will turn our attention to actually loving others with the love of Christ. In 1 Thessalonians 5:14 Paul provides us with an outline for exactly how we are to love others like Christ. There he tells us, "Now we exhort you, brethren, warn them that are unruly, comfort the feebleminded, support the weak ..." The love of Christ includes the elements of warning the unruly, comforting the feebleminded, and supporting the weak in the

> 1 Thessalonians 5:14
>
> Now we exhort you, brethren, warn them that are unruly, comfort the feebleminded, support the weak ...

faith. These are what we may refer to as the relational skills needed to develop and maintain healthy relationships at home, on the job, or in the community. Since they are expressions of divine love these relational skills generally define what it means for us to love others the way Christ does. Just as the communication skills were built upon the personal skills, so also are the relational skills are also built on both the personal and communication skills we have discussed. Our high calling of God in Christ Jesus is to love others the way he does. I call it the "critical event" because no matter what else we may do or say in our relationships to others it is critical that we love them.

The exercise of these relational skills may also be referred to as relational ministry. In modern Christianity we have a tendency to minimize our relationships in favor of rituals or beliefs. This is especially true in the church world where success tends to be measured by attendance at worship services, the number of programs offered, and, of course, the size of the budget. Unfortunately, ministry is usually defined by the performance of religious rituals and activities by professional "ministers" with the appropriate credentials, and relationships are often based on doctrines or a particular set of beliefs. Unity of the Spirit is often replaced by uniformity among the membership and compliance with the organizational norms. Within such religious organizations the quality of relationships often takes second place to the quality of the music and other forms of religious entertainment.

Even a casual reading of the New Testament, however, reveals the importance of divine love and the priority of relational ministry in the church. Of particular interest is Paul's overview of the goals and objectives for the leadership given in Ephesians 4:11-16.

> *"And he gave some apostles, and some prophets, and some, evangelists; and some, pastors and teachers; For the perfecting of the saints, for the work of the ministry, for the edifying of the body of Christ: Till we all come in the unity of the faith, and the knowledge of the Son of God, unto a perfect man, unto the measure of the stature of the fullness of Christ: That we henceforth be no more children, tossed to and fro, and carried about with every wind of doctrine, by the sleight of men, and the cunning craftiness whereby they lie in wait to deceive; But speaking the truth in love, may grow up unto him in all things, which is the head, even Christ; From whom*

the whole body fitly joined together and compacted by that which every joint supplieth, according to the effectual working in the measure of every part, maketh increase of the body unto the edifying of itself in love."

In these verses Paul reveals God's plan in providing gifted men to prepare the saints (all believers called of God for his use) for their ministry of edifying or build up the body of Christ (the church). Note that he does not say that these gifted men are to do the ministry of the church, but rather to equip the saints to do the ministry. The work of the ministry is what we are calling the critical event or simply relational ministry. At its core "the work of the ministry" is to love others like Christ in the very concrete and tangible ways we will describe as relational skills.

This ministry is to continue "till we all come in the unity of the faith" and mature into the fullness of Christ. In other words, the ultimate goal of relational ministry is to help others learn their true identity and potential in Christ so that they are no longer susceptible to religious deception and game playing. By "speaking the truth in love" our relational ministry to others will allow them to find their legitimate place as a member of the body of Christ (discover they are "fitly joined"), improve their relationships with others ("compacted by that which every joint supplieth"), and engage in their own relational ministry ("maketh increase of the body unto the edifying of itself in love"). Clearly, the role of relational ministry in the church is of the utmost importance as far as Paul is concerned. No amount of "religious entertainment" in a Sunday morning church service can substitute for preparing believers to engage in their ministry of loving others like Christ. No matter how eloquent the preacher, how big the offering, or how sweet the music, without the critical event of the saints loving each other we have missed the point of church altogether. Loving others like Christ means that we are going to warn those who are unruly, comfort them when they are hurting, and support them when they are weak in the faith.

Warn the Unruly

The first aspect of relational ministry we are called to is confrontational in nature. The phrase, "warn them that are unruly," refers to the job of confronting those who are behaving inappropriately. The idea is to love others enough to get involved with them when we see them doing things that are harmful to themselves and others. Likewise, we are to warn those who are not doing the things that are necessary for the welfare of themselves or others. The word translated, "warn" comes from a Greek word that literally means, "to put in mind" implying that our warning is to have an impact on the person's thinking. As noted earlier, the only way to really change a person's behavior is to effect a change in the thinking. That is, changes in their false assumptions and beliefs about themselves, God, and others are required for lasting changes in their behavior. The relational skill of warning the unruly, then, must involve helping them identify and change their minds.

The same basic thought is expressed in Galatians 6:1, *"Brethren, if a man be overtaken in a fault, ye which are spiritual, restore such a one in the spirit of meekness; considering thyself, lest thou also be tempted."* The goal of this relational ministry is not simply confrontation, but ultimately restoration. Restoration involves not only changing inappropriate and dysfunctional behavior, but also requires a change in thinking and feeling. Warning the unruly is not a simple and quick fix, but a time consuming commitment. To be effective in this ministry it is

> Galatians 6:1
> Brethren, if a man be overtaken in a fault, ye which are spiritual, restore such a one in the spirit of meekness; considering thyself, lest thou also be tempted.

absolutely necessary to be controlled by the Spirit and motivated by divine love.

In order to engage in the ministry of removing the "splinter" from our brother's eye we are going to have to get rid of the judgmental "beam" in our own. Like the other two relational skills, warning the unruly demands a healthy self examination and honesty with ourselves, God, and those we seek to restore. This aspect of relational ministry requires the intelligent love of God that does what is best for the one loved, not what will make them feel good. A more detailed discussion of the ministry of warning the unruly will follow in the next chapter. For now, note that such a ministry is not reserved only for the professional clergy, counselors, or civil authorities, but is the responsibility of the "brethren." All believers are charged with the responsibility of being used by God to confront and restore those who are not behaving appropriately. We cannot avoid that responsibility, with its accompanying discomfort, by paying "professionals" to do our ministry, "They're paid to do that, it's not my job!" is really a religious cop out that may sound good to our fellow man, but not to the Lord.

Comfort the Feebleminded

The second aspect of relational ministry has to do with comforting those who are "feebleminded" or emotionally distraught. We are not simply to concern ourselves with the behavior of others but with their emotions as well. Those around us who are struggling with personal issues, family crisis, financial problems, etc., are in desperate need of people who understand and can accept their feelings. They do not need theological information as much as a warm smile or a friendly hug. This relational skill is also vital to restoration.

Simply being present with those who are suffering offers more comfort than eloquent speeches and the great philosophies of men. In 2 Corinthians Paul tells us where our comfort comes from and how we can actually comfort others. In the first chapter he says,

> 2 Corinthians
>
> Blessed be God, even the Father of our Lord Jesus Christ, the Father of mercies, and the God of all comfort; Who comforteth us in all our tribulation, that we may be able to comfort them which are in any trouble, by the comfort wherewith we our-selves are comforted of God.

"Blessed be God, even the Father of our Lord Jesus Christ, the Father of mercies, and the God of all comfort; Who comforteth us in all our tribulation, that we may be able to comfort them which are in any trouble, by the comfort wherewith we ourselves are comforted of God". The comfort we have to offer to others is the comfort we have received from God by believing the gospel in the middle of our own trials. Our willingness to be present with those who are suffering sets the stage for the Comforter to use us to comfort others.

No one naturally enjoys hanging out with people who are hurting. It puts us in an awkward position of not knowing what to say or do to relieve their suffering and ease the pain. But as we are willing to "weep with those who weep" the Comforter gives us what we need at the time to be present with the hurting. Although much more will be said later, it is enough for now to understand it's not what we say that counts as much as it is just being present. Remember, actions speak louder than words, especially in times of suffering. Our willingness to be present says, "I love you" and brings comfort to the hurting like nothing else can do.

Support the Weak

The third relational skill involves supporting those who are weak in the faith. These folks have trouble believing the gospel for themselves, never mind others. It is easy to confuse those who are "weak in the faith" with the "feeble-minded' since they both have a lot of pain and tend to do a lot of whining. The telltale sign, however, is that the weak rarely think of what God has done for them in Christ to make them secure and significant, and are usually busy trying to prove themselves "worthy" in their own eyes. As a result, the weak in the faith tend to be very religious and are often quite obnoxious at the same time. They are usually very legalistic in their thinking and are likely to spend their time criticizing others or condemning themselves.

Our natural reaction to such people is to avoid them at all costs. We try to stay away from their negative outlook and critical spirit knowing that it could just as easily turn on us. When they judge, criticize, and gossip about others we may be tempted to join them at first, but often find ourselves looking for a convenient way to avoid them. After an episode of criticism the weak in the faith will usually start condemning themselves. Their self deprecating words and attitude are motivated by a false humility meant to solicit pity from those around them. They identify themselves as "victims" that have a right to criticize others and adopt the "martyr role" to gain approval from others. Naturally, we want to keep our exposure to such people to a minimum.

In Romans 14:1, however, Paul instructs us who are "strong in the faith" to *receive* those who are "weak in the faith" and not trouble them about their "doubtful issues." The "doubtful issues" are simply those issues in our lives that the Bible does not directly address. The weak in the faith will seek to make up rules about such things and impose them on themselves and others as a standard for being a "good" Christian. The subject of most of their complaining and whining will be about others not believing, feeling, or acting the way they do concerning those doubtful issues. The difficult part of supporting those who are weak is in accepting them in spite of their critical spirit and judgmental attitudes.

The relational skill of supporting the weak in the faith, in many ways, is more difficult than confronting or comforting others. Accepting them as worthy persons despite their religious and obnoxious flesh is sometimes a real challenge. The way we do this is to see him through the eyes of our Savior. This requires mountain-moving faith on our part. We must use the eyes of faith to look through his religious facade to see a worthy but frightened child of God who really isn't sure that he is truly accepted by the Father. We must believe the gospel that he is secure in God's love and significant in God's eternal plan whether he believes so or not. In so doing, we can relate to him in such a way as to encourage and stimulate his faith in the gospel for himself.

Summary

The relational skills of warning the unruly, comforting the feeble-minded, and supporting the weak are the tools we need to be able to fulfill our high calling of God to love others like Christ. This is the relational ministry every believer is called to as their central purpose in this life. It is the job of spiritual leadership in the church to equip the saints for this vital ministry among its membership. We have not been left here on earth as mere spectators to be entertained or ministered to by others, but to serve others in love. Our true goal in life is not to make ourselves look and feel good, but to serve others around us. These relational skills are simply three aspects of loving someone like Christ enough to confront them, comfort them, and support them.

Although we may think of theses skills as being applied to three different types of people, they are usually needed to love the same person throughout the relationship. For example, confronting inappropriate behavior, comforting those who are suffering, and supporting the weak are skills that every parent needs to raise their children. Any lasting relationship will require the use of all three of these skills at some time or another if it is to be based on the love of Christ.

Exercises

1. Identify and describe a relational situation in which you saw the need to confront someone who was behaving inappropriately. Chances are you were offended personally by their behavior (what they said or did in that situation) and wanted to see them change. Ask yourself two important questions about this situation: first, "why do I want them to change?" and second, "what is the Spirit telling me to do or say to restore them in love?"

2. Describe another situation in which you related to someone who was hurting emotionally. Describe their feelings and what you felt you needed to do about them. Describe how you tried to deal with their pain and the outcome of you efforts.

3. Think of a situation in which you tried to relate to someone who was negative, whining, and critical of others. Describe any efforts you made in talking to them and note how easy it was for you to "get on the band wagon" with them. Identify why they were so negative and critical of others, perhaps even you.

4. Those seeking true recovery will make a list of people they have harmed or offended in their dysfunction; and where possible they will try to make amends. Make your list of people you may have offended and include those who may have offended you and identify the relations skills you will need to make amends.

II. Confrontation without Condemnation

The first relational skill we need to consider is that of confronting inappropriate behavior in others without condemning them. Learning to confront without condemnation requires the use of all the personal and communications skills discussed earlier. All relationships will, sooner or later, require this relational skill because we all exhibit the flesh on a regular basis. Jesus warned his disciples about this natural tendency toward interpersonal strife when he said, "Woe unto the world because of offenses, for it must needs be that offenses come." (Matthew 18). Jesus knew that living in a sin-cursed body that still has the flesh, with others who also have the flesh, was not going to be easy. He knew that we were going to face personal conflict in this world and wanted his disciples to learn how to cope with it.

In that context Jesus went on to teach his disciples to deal with the hatred of their own flesh before going on to address their responsibility to confront the offending party. In essence he told them to take "time out to do a trip in" as we have discussed earlier. Only when we take the time to allow God deal with our flesh are we prepared to deal with the flesh of others in a useful and constructive manner. Any confrontation designed to whine about the offense to a sympathetic ear or to seek revenge for the offense will end up in condemnation rather than restoration. The goal of this relational skill reaches beyond simply complaining about or manipulating the offender...it seeks to restore them.

When to Confront? - Timing

The first issue to consider is knowing when it is necessary to warn or confront one who is unruly or behaving inappropriately. Just because we may actually observe inappropriate behavior does not necessarily mean that we must confront the unruly one. There is much work that needs to be done on our part in applying the principles of the personal skills first.

> Galatians 6:1
>
> Brothers, if a man is overtaken in a fault, you the spiritual ones restore such a one in the spirit of meekness, considering yourself, lest you also be tempted.

For instance, a parent may notice their adolescent child has not completed their household chores and is hanging out with their friends instead. Just because we notice inappropriate behavior does not mean that we are prepared or required to confront the child immediately. Unruly or inappropriate behavior by itself is not what determines the timing of our response. The command of Paul in Galatians 6:1 to restore them does not mean we must immediately confront their behavior, but rather reveals that we have some personal work that needs to be done in us in order to restore them. The most critical part of this preparation is the personal leadership of the Spirit, not the least of which is the timing in confronting others to restore them.

The key phrase in Paul's command to restore the one overtaken in a fault is, "you who are spiritual restore such a one..." This means you who are being controlled by the Spirit are to do the restoring. Only those who are prepared and led by the Spirit should engage in warning the unruly and seeking restoration. Without the necessary spiritual enlightenment we run a high risk of simply reacting to the inappropriate behavior with our own knowledge of good and evil. The result of such a reaction in the religious flesh is to complicate the problem by either co-dependant enabling or total condemnation. In short, without the leadership and power of the Spirit we will likely make the situation worse. Experience tells us that simply observing the unruly behavior and discerning the dangers associated with it does not mean that we must say or do something about it right away. Waiting on the prompting of the Spirit within is critical to the ministry of restoration. Our immediate reaction to unruly behavior should be prayer rather than confrontation. Like Jesus, we can pray, "Father forgive them, for they know not what they do" and allow the Spirit to tell us when it is time to confront.

Why Confront? - Motivation

While we wait on the leadership of the Spirit we are not simply ignoring the problem. Applying the personal skills learned earlier, we would seek the spiritual enlightenment necessary to evaluate our own goals, manage our own emotions, and restructure our own thinking before we actually confront the unruly person. What is my goal in confronting? Is it ministry or manipulation? Am I seeking to love them by what I am about to say, or do I want to manipulate and control them somehow? What am I feeling right now? Is it anger tempered with divine love, or is it bitterness and hatred? What do I believe about myself? Do I believe that I must make them behave to make myself worthy, or do I believe that I am worthy regardless of their behavior? All these questions need to be answered in our own minds before we confront the unruly; otherwise, we run the risk of becoming part of the problem rather than part of the solution.

This is where the communication skills of taking time out for the trip in are needed. Remember, we need to talk with God before we try to talk to others, especially the unruly. And what we need to talk with him about is our own beliefs, emotions, and behavior in this situation. Whenever we observe unruly behavior in another, especially those close to us, our flesh will naturally raise its ugly self in terms of false assumptions about our own worth, negative emotions quickly turning to destructive emotions, and the selfish motivations of fear, guilt, and pride robbing our faith, hope , and love.

Most likely the unruly behavior will present a threat to our own sense of worth causing us to doubt our own security and significance. Such doubt produces feelings of hatred, self-pity, and anxiety which we naturally try to deny or distort because we "know better". Our verbal and non-verbal behavior at that point is motivated by fear, guilt, and pride so that we are essentially neutralized by our own issues and cannot be effective in restoring the unruly one. And all this happens in a matter of minutes, or seconds! This is why it is so important to take time for the trip in.

When led by the Spirit of Truth, the trip in will expose all the motivations, feelings, and false assumptions of our flesh. It's not a pretty picture, but looking at it is necessary for us to be honest with God and agree with him that it is there. Such confession of our sins will be rewarded by the promise that he is faithful and just to forgive our sins and cleanse us from all unrighteousness. The forgiveness we receive from God is what we have to share with others.

Earl tried all his life to forgive his grandmother. His father had abandoned the family shortly after he was born and his mother had to work two jobs just to make ends meet. Earl, a rambunctious boy, was cared for by his grandmother who apparently was from the "old school" when it came to discipline. When Earl acted out she felt the best way to deal with him was to put him in a burlap sack and beat him with a stick till he quit crying. Naturally, Earl grew up hating his grandmother and learned to stuff that hatred down inside. But, like all festering hatred, it could not be contained. It continued to grow and to spill over to his mother for leaving him with grandma, his unknown father for abandoning the family, and God for permitting the whole thing to happen. Being a Christian Earl had tried many times to forgive his grandma, but it was a perpetual struggle.

Despite the abuse, Earl grew up and had his own family, a wife and two children. For a while he thought he had overcome his past by working hard to provide for his family and being a good father to his children. But to Earl's surprise, he found it more and more difficult to keep a lid on his hatred, especially when he had a couple drinks after work. Finally, Earl became so abusive he was arrested and sent to a rehab center. One day in group therapy Earl got honest about his lifelong struggle with hatred. He broke down in tears and stated that he just couldn't forgive his grandma and, to make matters worse, she had passed on so he couldn't even confront her.

In order for Earl to be able to love his family he had to learn about and experience the forgiveness of God. Since he was an innocent child when he was abused, Earl was surprised when asked if he had received forgiveness in his situation. What Earl had not realized was that his own hatred toward his grandma and others was just as much a sin as their abuse. He didn't realize that you have to receive forgiveness before you can give it. You cannot give what you do not have. Citing the example of Jesus who prayed forgiveness for the very men crucifying him, Earl was asked to simply ask God to forgive his hatred so that he could forgive like Christ. That day Earl did a life changing trip in and experienced God sending all his hatred away so that he could forgive others, even his dead grandmother.

While Earl's case may be somewhat extreme it is nonetheless all too common. We all have similar issues of the flesh requiring divine intervention. This is the "beam" Jesus said we need to remove from our own eyes before we are able to take the "splinter" out of the eye of others. Taking the time for the trip in is absolutely necessary before we confront those who are behaving inappropriately.

Restoration or Condemnation?

Depending on what we find when we consider our own beliefs, emotions, and motives, we may be surprised to learn that our real goal in confrontation is simply condemnation rather than restoration. It is so much easier to condemn than to restore. All we have to do is find an appropriate rule or law that prohibits the behavior in question, prove that it is inappropriate, and find the offender guilty. But such condemnation will neither change the behavior nor build healthy relationships. As a matter of fact, it has a tendency to increase the likelihood of further acting out and ultimately destroys relationships. Are we most interested in establishing guilt or restoration? The only legitimate goal for confrontation is that of restoration.

At this point it is necessary to establish a *key point*. If we are not willing to invest the time and energy required to follow through with the other relational skills of comfort and support, then confrontation is best left undone. Confrontation without a genuine commitment to restoration will be perceived as condemnation. Restoration requires a costly commitment to help the offender behave appropriately with their personal needs fully met. In short, condemnation is quick and easy, requires no commitment on our part, and may even produce temporary outward compliance if severe enough. Restoration, on the other hand, requires a long-term commitment to spend whatever time and energy is necessary to address the personal needs and change the belief systems of the one confronted.

Like all other forms of ministry, the relational ministry of restoring those who are overtaken in a fault is not something that can be done quickly. Many well meaning, but naive Christians have set themselves up for failure by thinking they can simply quote a few relevant Bible verses, pray a quick prayer, or perform a religious ritual to restore the unruly. While they may seem to enjoy a measure of success as the unruly allows them to perform and may even thank them for their efforts, they are soon surprised and discouraged by the inevitable relapse. At that point, they are faced with a difficult choice…they must decide who is to be blamed for the obvious failure, their own "ministry" efforts, or the unruly one that relapsed. The ministry of restoration requires a long-term commitment involving the relational skills of comfort and support as well as confrontation.

Behavioral Modification Is Not Enough

In seeking to confront inappropriate behavior we naturally want to see that behavior changed or modified in some fashion. To do so, however, requires a fundamental change in the thoughts and, to some extent, the feelings of the one we want to change. Specifically, the desired change in behavior must come from the inside rather than the outside. That is, the initial goal of confrontation is to begin the dialogue necessary to help the other change the way they think about themselves and their own needs, not just their behavior.

Most people, especially children, are not aware of their own personal needs for unconditional love and genuine respect. Neither are they aware that their daily behavior is determined by what they believe will meet those needs in the most efficient way. Inappropriate behavior, no matter how irrational and irresponsible it may seem, has an underlying belief system concerning the way these needs will be met that locks the behavior in place. In other words, people behave in the manner they think has the best possibility of a personal pay-off for them. The pay-off is always some form of getting their personal needs met. While we may use various external means of modifying the behavior (i.e. positive or negative reinforcement, positive or negative punishment) any observable change is usually temporary unless the underlying belief systems are changed.

> People behave in the manner they think has the best possibility of a personal pay-off for them.

Mowing the weeds in the lawn may improve the looks of the lawn temporarily, but we must deal with the roots to get rid of the weeds permanently. Children as well as parents must learn the personal skill of cognitive restructuring in order to change their inappropriate behavior. For example, the adolescent girl who is acting out sexually must learn to identify the personal needs she is trying to meet and the false beliefs that lead her to use sex as a means to gratify those needs. To condemn her as a person and punish her with restriction may change her behavior temporarily, but teaching her a better way to get her needs met is required for any permanent change.

People engaged in inappropriate behavior are not doing so simply because they "don't know the rules" or are somehow unaware of the ultimate consequences of their unruly behavior. Neither do they act inappropriately because they simply choose to do so. Their behavior is built upon the underlying belief structures concerning what they think will satisfy their deepest personal needs. As the proverb says, "As a man thinketh in his heart, so is he". Confrontation with the goal of restoration will involve challenging the belief systems and learning the skill of cognitive restructuring.

> Confrontation with the goal of restoration will involve challenging the belief systems and learning the skill of cognitive restructuring.

structuring rather than simply modifying behavior. This takes time and energy we must be willing to sacrifice for the welfare of those we seek to restore.

The Identity Factor

Successful confrontation requires making a distinction in our own minds between the person and their behavior and helping them recognize their true identity. In confronting a person who is lying, we must not fall prey to the common belief that those who lie are "liars". Equating personal identity with behavior is not only a lie, but also entrenches the behavior. The specific change in thinking that must

> Equating personal identity with behavior is not only a lie, but also entrenches the behavior.

occur for a permanent change in behavior is a change in personal identity.

Our beliefs about our personal identity (who we think we are), determine how we feel about ourselves and, to a large extent, what we are likely to do. A person who believes he is worthless will naturally feel insecure (unloved and disrespected) and is more likely to act worthless because of his false identity. Very often his evidence for such a worthless self-image is his own performance, which is only reinforced when others equate his person with his worthless performance.

Effective confrontation of inappropriate behavior includes some sort of challenge to the faulty identity underlying the behavior. For instance, confronting a person who has been caught shoplifting may include a statement such as, "I don't think you really are a thief even though you are behaving like one. You must have problems acting like who you really are. You obviously don't know who you really are since you have been acting like someone else, and not the real person you are." Statements like, "This proves that you are nothing but a thief!" will do nothing but reinforce the behavior of shoplifting. While the one confronted must face the consequences of their inappropriate behavior, it is extremely important to challenge the false identity underneath that behavior.

The key to the identify factor is to understand the difference between a true identity and a false identity. The only true identity anyone has is what God has made us to be. In the Bible, he says we are just like Jesus Christ, not behaviorally, but relationally. Anything less is a false identity. The goal of restoration for all who behave inappropriately is to replace the false identity with the true. This is not an act of behavioral modification but rather, a change in identity, which is seen in the Scriptures as simple death and resurrection. The sexually active girl must see herself as worthy as Christ and understand her identity in a relationship with him before she can really change her behavior. She must understand that she is a new creation, that the person she once was no longer exists and a new person who is perfect and without blemish before God has taken her place. A death and a resurrection have occurred. The person shoplifting needs to view himself as having the character of Christ before he can quit stealing from others.

Replacing the false identity with the new requires two things. First, someone has to tell the one being confronted about his or her true identity. How can we possibly believe in something we have never heard? This involves much more that a simple lecture that sounds like some sort of sermon. It demands a genuine belief in that true identity on the part of the one confronting. The idea here is not, "You can be worthy if you quit having sex, or stop shoplifting" but rather, "You are worthy because God made you just like Jesus, never mind the fact that you are not acting worthy by having sex or shoplifting… you are, in fact, worthy!" Your identity is secure with God regardless of your behavior, past, present, or future.

Second, the one being confronted must want to believe their true identity rather than the false. This does not mean that they must somehow convince themselves or that we must convince them of their true identity, but rather they must have a genuine desire to have God convince them through his spiritual enlightenment. The only thing we may do is to believe it for them and demonstrate our faith by expressing divine love in all that we do or say. It is important to note at this point that there is no guarantee that the one we confront will change their thinking or their behavior. A genuine expression of divine love may include that which is referred to as "tough love."

For example, a wife may confront her husband about an extramarital affair that has been denied for some time. If her husband refuses to change his thinking and thus his behavior, she is left no choice but to "let him go" by filing for divorce. Seeking a divorce may not look like divine love, but it is necessary to stop enabling him in his fantasy of "having his cake and eating it too." We often refer to this as a "wake-up call." Likewise, parents who confront their adolescent boy about his drug abuse may actually have to cut off all financial and physical support to express genuine love if he is not willing to change from the inside out. Knowing when to file for divorce, call the authorities, put them out of the house, or simply say no to their manipulation requires the spiritual enlightenment spoken of earlier. No one but God knows the best way to "tough love" a rebellious child or a dysfunctional spouse. Often we so desperately want to help our family members and others that we will jeopardize ourselves and others in the family to do so. Listening to the inner voice of the Spirit tell us when and where to draw the line is the only healthy way to find our answer. However, that inner voice must be the Spirit and not our own desire, led by our own need for having our personal needs satisfied.

The relational skill of confronting inappropriate behavior sounds much more complex than it really is. When we make it our goal to love our family members and others in this important way we are actually entering into relational ministry. The one guaranteed prayer request Jesus gave his disciple was in the context of ministering to the needs of others, "Whatever you ask in my name, that will I do that the Father may be glorified." It is our willingness to be used of God to love those we must confront that gives us the power to restore them. It is their willingness to believe the truth about their true identity that gives them the power to change. Although it may all sound so complex, it is really simple enough for anyone to do.

Summary

Confrontation without condemnation is a vital part of loving others like Christ. As Jesus pointed out this relational skill is necessary because there will always be times of interpersonal strife and conflict in any relationship. Paul summarizes our ministry at such times with the call to warn the unruly and restore them, "in a spirit of meekness, considering yourself lest ye be also tempted." Our temptation will be not to engage. This is the same dysfunctional behavior, but to judge and condemn them rather than love them despite their actions. We "consider ourselves" by taking time to do the trip in and allowing the Spirit not only to prepare us, but also to lead and empower us.

Jesus likewise instructed his disciples to deal with offenses by first dealing with their own hatred (which is like cutting off your own hand or poking out you own eye) before we go to the one who offended us. A failure to do the trip in and be led by the Spirit will always end in more hurt feelings and confusion. It is just as likely for the Spirit to lead us in simply forgiving the offending one as it is to be led to restore them. Restoration demands a much higher level of commitment to relational ministry and is reserved for those that God specifically calls and empowers to get the job done.

Exercises

1. The first step in exercising the relational skill of confrontation is to recognize the personal leadership of the Spirit. Think of a situation in which you recognized someone behaving inappropriately and ask your self what the Spirit was leading you to do.
2. Most of the time the Spirit will lead us to simply forgive the one overtaken in a fault rather than confront him. Why?
3. Describe a situation in which you think the Spirit was leading you to warn the unruly. Describe the relational history you have with that person. What have you done to show that person you loved them and were committed to restoring them, not simply condemning them?
4. Considering yourself means taking the trip in to evaluate your own behavior, emotions, and beliefs before you seek to warn the unruly. Give an example of how your trip in prepared you to confront another without condemning them.

12. Encouragement without Enabling

There is no lack of hurting people in our world today. When we get outside of ourselves long enough to look at those around us, it is obvious that, even in the richest and most powerful nation in the world, there are many people suffering. In order to love others like Christ we are going to have to meet them where they are…and that usually means coping with suffering to one degree or another. Suffering is relative, meaning that one person may suffer more than another according to their own particular circumstances. But to the one hurting, suffering is suffering regardless the cause or how severe it may be. To love others like Christ involves a willingness on our part to comfort them in the midst of their pain.

The relational skill of comforting those who are hurting also usually follows quickly on the heels of confrontation. Although there are times when we may comfort people for other reasons, often it is in association with having confronted their behavior. In either case, the goal of this skill is to help them manage their emotions in a healthy way. Like the relational skill of warning the unruly, comforting the feebleminded is developed from exercising the personal and communication skills. This means that there is just as much need for the personal preparation and the power of the Spirit for this ministry of love as there is for the relational ministry of confrontation.

The Call to Comfort

Right from the beginning of his second letter to the Corinthian church the apostle Paul describes our call to comfort the feebleminded or those who are hurting. *"Blessed be God, even the Father of our Lord Jesus Christ, the Father of mercies, and the God of all comfort; Who comforteth us in all our tribulation, that we may be able to comfort them which are in any trouble, by the comfort wherewith we ourselves are comforted of God."* Notice that Paul begins this "ministry training" letter with the call to comfort others. This seems to emphasize that our ministry to others will always involve comforting them to some degree. Here he refers to God as the "Father of mercies, and the God of all comfort"; which also strongly

> **2 Corinthians**
> Blessed be God, even the Father of our Lord Jesus Christ, the Father of mercies, and the God of all comfort; Who comforteth us in all our tribulation, that we may be able to comfort them which are in any trouble, by the comfort wherewith we ourselves are comforted of God.

implies that any service we offer to others will have something to do with extending mercy and comfort to those who fail and are suffering. The scope of this relational ministry is not restricted to those we may deem as worthy, but includes even those we may think are deserving of their pain.

The call to comfort others is linked directly to God's comfort in our own lives. Paul states unequivocally that we are comforted of God in all our tribulation. This means that God is actively working to comfort us every time we suffer, whether we perceive it or not. As will be discussed later, the moment we experience any kind of tribulation the indwelling Spirit of God goes to work making intercession for us and producing the character of Christ in us. The comfort we receive in our own lives is given us by the God of mercies and all comfort so that we may share that same comfort with others. The preparation needed to engage in this relational ministry of comforting the feebleminded is provided by God himself. To develop this relational skill then means that we learn a healthy way to cope with our own suffering, so that we may be used of God to help others.

The real test of our faith in the gospel of Jesus Christ always involves personal suffering. Nothing causes us to doubt our worth as persons as much as the personal trials we are called upon to endure in this world. In the first half of Romans 8, Paul reveals the glorious gospel of God's provisions in the Spirit to set us free from the habit and power of sin. Based upon our union with Christ, we are under no condemnation, and are free from guilt, free from feeling guilty, free from fear, able to relate to God with the boldness and confidence of his child, and fully equipped. We enjoy the blessings of the freedom, mind, power, leadership and assurance of the Holy Spirit. Since we are the adopted children of God, we are joint-heirs with Christ. What a glorious privilege to be one with Jesus!

In the middle of verse 17, however, Paul introduces the fact that we are joint-heirs with Christ, "if so be that we suffer with him, that we may be also glorified together." He connects our glory and rejoicing in Christ with our suffering with Him. Our wonderful union with Christ involves His sufferings as well as His blessings. In making this connection Paul raises the one issue that causes us to doubt the gospel we have been studying —personal suffering; and then he goes on to describe the comfort God gives us in all our tribulations so that we my comfort others.

> **Romans 8:17**
>
> And if we are children, then we are heirs; heirs of God and joint-heirs with Christ; so that if we suffer with *Him*, we may also be glorified together.

The Eternal View of Suffering

Normally, we are more concerned about why we suffer than we are the comfort of God in our suffering. Our fleshly thinking is focused on "why did this happen to me" in an effort to protect ourselves. Seeking to rationalize and justify the suffering we often fail to accept the comfort of God when we need it most. It is because of this kind of thinking that Paul refers to the ones we are to comfort as the "feebleminded". Not having the experience of being comforted of God, we waste a lot of time and energy in asking why bad things happen to us instead of looking for the comfort God has promised when we do.

Paul addresses this age old question in the latter half of Romans 8. Before stating why we must suffer, he reveals the astounding truth, *"...the sufferings of this present time are not worthy to be compared with the glory which shall be revealed in us."* Believing this connection between our suffering and our glory, however, demands an eternal view of our suffering that can only be viewed from God's perspective. That is, we must learn to see, by faith, the end result of our suffering at the beginning of it. God's comfort in our suffering only comes through an exercise of faith in the eternal view of our suffering.

In Romans 5:1-5, Paul introduces us to this "eternal view" by outlining the benefits of being justified by faith in Jesus. In addition to peace with God, access into His grace, and rejoicing in the hope of our final destiny in glory; he goes on to outline the unique way we may face our trials and tribulations. Instead of dreading them, we can actually glory or rejoice in them knowing that tribula-

> **Romans 5:1-5**
>
> Therefore being justified by faith, we have peace with God through our Lord Jesus Christ.
>
> Through Him we also have access by faith into this grace in which we stand, and we rejoice on the hope of the glory of God.
>
> And not only *this*, but we glory in afflictions also, knowing that afflictions work out patience, and patience *works out* experience, and experience *works out* hope.
>
> And hope does not make *us* ashamed, because the love of God has been poured out in our hearts through *the* Holy Spirit given to us.

tion produces patience, patience produces experience, experience produces hope, and hope never lets us down because God loves us as His own.

When we see our sufferings from the eternal viewpoint of our union with Christ, we can see the end from the beginning, and know that *"...the sufferings of this present time are not worthy to be compared with the glory which shall be revealed in us."* Whatever we must suffer in this life cannot even be compared to the glory and rejoicing that awaits us. As he explains in 2 Corinthians 4, *"For our light affliction, which is but for a moment, worketh for us a far more exceeding and eternal weight of glory; While we look not at the things which are seen, but at the things which are not seen: for the things which are seen are temporal; but the things which are not seen are eternal".* Learning to receive the comfort God provides for us in our suffering is vital, not only to provide us with the comfort we need, but also to prepare us to be able to comfort others.

> **2 Corinthians 4**
>
> *For our light affliction, which is but for a moment, worketh for us a far more exceeding and eternal weight of glory; While we look not at the things which are seen, but at the things which are not seen: for the things which are seen are temporal; but the things which are not seen are eternal*

The following chart summarizes the eternal view of suffering revealed in the scriptures that offers us the comfort of God.

We should not be surprised when we suffer seeing that we are living in a sin-cursed world in sin-cursed bodies that are falling apart. Living in such conditions guarantees we, like the creation itself, "groan within ourselves" in suffering and pain. A significant part of our surprise when we suffer is connected to the religious "deal" we often make with God. That deal goes something like this, "God, I promise to try as hard as I can to be a good Christian , and you don't let anything bad happen to me or my loved ones." The

THE ETERNAL VIEW OF SUFFERING

DO NOT BE SURPRISED   (1 Peter 4:12-14)
—Because of union with Christ   (John 15:18)
—For the sake of Christ   (Phil. 1:27)
—As a testimony to others   (1 Peter 3:13)

SEE THE END AT THE BEGINNING   (2 Cor. 4:17-18)
—God's love   (Romans 5:3-5)
—Joy unspeakable   (1 Peter 1:3-9)
—Peaceable fruit of righteousness   (Hebrews 12:1-11)
—Spiritual maturity   (James 1:2-4)

KNOW YOU CANNOT LOSE   (1 John 5:4)
—With trial comes grace   (2 Cor. 10:13)
—God is in absolute control   (1 Cor. 10:13)
—All things work for good   (Romans 8:28)
—More than conquerors   (Romans 8:37)

problem is God doesn't make deals like that. No one in the history of humanity was ever more obedient or pleasing to God than Jesus. And yet no one suffered more than he. While it is true that God could simply take us out of this world as soon as we are born again, he has chosen to leave us in these sin-cursed bodies, in a sin-cursed world, as ambassadors for Christ. We should not be at all surprised, then, when we suffer in this present time. Rather than spend our time trying to avoid suffering and whining about it when it happens, we need to be able to receive the comfort God promises to give us.

Jesus received this comfort of God as he suffered in this world. The writer of Hebrews tells us, "Wherefore seeing we also are compassed about with so great a cloud of witnesses, let us lay aside every weight, and the sin which doth so easily beset us, and let us run with patience the race that is set before us, Looking unto Jesus the author and finisher of our faith; who for the joy that was set before him endured the cross, despising the shame, and is set down at the right hand of the throne of God." The "joy that was set before him" was the comfort of God he received to enable him to go through the suffering, not avoid it. The same comfort that allowed him to fulfill his ministry on the cross is what God promises to give each of us when we suffer.

Before seeking to comfort others it is important for us to learn to receive that comfort ourselves. The personal skill of emotional management must be practiced by the one seeking to comfort others who are hurting (i.e. fully acknowledging our feelings to God, allowing Him to affirm our own worth, and committing ourselves to serving others). The comfort we are going to share with others must first be received by us, since we cannot give what we do not have. This is especially true when seeking to comfort our own family members and close friends. Only when God comforts us by affirming our true identity and worth as persons can we pass on that same comfort to others.

Comforting Others

The most difficult part of comforting others is that we must learn to accept rather than reject their hurt feelings. This means we must listen to them rather than lecture them. Although we may have some tremendous wisdom and insight to share with those who are hurting, we need to first learn to accept their emotional pain rather than quickly try to fix them. When comforting others, it is usually far more important to simply listen to them and cry with them than it is to suggest a possible solution to their suffering. Our willingness to "weep with those who weep" is far more important than coming up with some words of wisdom. Because feelings are the most personal things we may share with others, we must not handle them as we would a bag of trash. We must allow them to express their feelings (good, bad, and ugly) without judging or condemning if we want to bring true comfort.

After we have earned the right to speak to them about their feelings by listening attentively, we may begin to share the truth that it's not just their situation that is causing their hurt, but what they are believing about themselves in that situation that really hurts their feelings. Underneath every hurt is a lie about our personal needs for

---

ABC Theory of Emotions

A. Bad things happen to us.
B. The lies about personal security and significance control our feelings of hate and anxiety.
C. Our hurts is based upon what we believe about ourselves.

---

worth. If we are going to comfort others in their pain we must be aware of the lies that produce that pain. Remember the ABC theory of emotions? It's not just event A (the bad things that happen to us) that determines how we feel (consequence C); the real culprit in our hurt is our own negative self-talk based on what we believe about ourselves (B). The lies about our personal security and significance (the love and respect we need daily) transform our anger into hatred, our hurt into self-pity, and our fears into anxiety. These subtle lies about our worth as persons must be challenged and replaced with the truth of our worthiness in order to cope with suffering in a healthy way.

For instance, a child may be hurt by the fact that he did not make the football team. After listening to him express his disappointment and pain over that situation, we might introduce the idea that his pain is made worse by a natural lie about his worth associated with the fact that he did not make the team. He may believe that he is less acceptable or less important because he did not make the team. His hurt will be magnified due to his believing that he is somehow worth less, and his comfort will involve recognizing and eliminating that lie. However, this is easier said than done. Teenagers are very complex, hormonal and influenced by peer pressure. Consequently there are many lies and overlapping lies that need to be confronted.

Helping others to recognize the lies about their own security and significance and affirm the truth of their personal worth is more of an art than a science.

> Helping others to recognize the lies about their own security and significance and affirm the truth of their personal worth is more of an art than it is a science.

There is no formula to follow that will fit all individuals, but we may be sure that all will have some sort of lie present. The main goal here is to simply challenge the lies about their worth and affirm the truth of the good news that they are, in fact, secure in God's love and significant in his plan. Sharing your own false assumptions about your worth as an example will likely encourage them toward recognizing and challenging theirs. Your personal honesty and transparency about the lies you must confront sets the example of the cognitive restructuring and emotional management they need to endure their own suffering. Such openness on your part tells them that you not only understand their pain, but also earns you the right to affirm the truth of their worth despite their suffering.

True comfort for those who are hurting must ultimately come from "the God of all comfort." Sometimes the pain and hurt is so intense that no amount of human encouragement really helps. After all is done to accept their feelings and the lies about their personal worth are challenged with the truth; only the Comforter, himself, can actually "renew" their minds and give them the needed comfort.

While God will certainly use you to comfort them, it is important to realize that only he can make that comfort real to them. Your job is to simply be present with them in their suffering, not to take away their pain…that's God's job. Setting the example of trusting God to comfort them, helping them recognize the lies about their worth as persons, and expressing your love and respect for them is as far as you can go. You cannot make them feel better by yourself…only the Comforter can do that.

What you can do is to help them recognize God's comfort and listen to them express how God is working in their lives. Typically, people who are suffering confuse God's comfort with the removal of their suffering by changing their circumstances. They often miss the comfort he is giving them in the midst of their trial because they expect him to end or remove the trial in order to give them relief. As was the case of Jesus, God's comfort does not come from "letting the cup pass", but in our submission to his will in spite of the suffering. Because we are joined to Christ in his sufferings as well as his victories, we should expect the Father to comfort us through our trials, not just by removing our trials. As Paul explained to the suffering Philippians, *"For unto you it is given in the behalf of Christ, not only to believe on him, but also to suffer for his sake"*. A great deal of comfort comes from the simple recognition that our suffering does not mean we are not the children of God, but is proof that we are , in fact, identified with Christ. It is useful to remind them of how God sees their true identity despite their current suffering. Applying this eternal perspective of suffering to the pain they are going through offers them great hope. Their faith in what the God of all comfort has to say about their suffering produces the hope needed to endure their pain and care about others around them.

Those we are seeking to comfort need to be reminded not to be surprised when they suffer. According to the Bible we do not suffer because we have been or are bad, but because we live in a world that is falling apart at the seams in physical bodies that are also falling apart. The removal of personal blame during suffering is a vital step in comforting those who hurt. The idea that "it's my fault" does tremendous damage to our sense of personal security and significance. This idea must be challenged. The fact is bad things happen to us because we live in a world that is continually falling apart whether or not we behave ourselves. Remember the example of Jesus. Even the suffering that results from our own mistakes is a consequence of the fact that we yet have the "flesh" living in this physical body and should not be taken to be a sign of personal condemnation.

Next we must help them adopt the "eternal view" of their suffering. This simply means we focus on the end result of their suffering at the beginning. While this point may seem to be a little too philosophical, the comfort that comes from it is worth the trouble. Seeing the end at the beginning is only possible when we move out of the physical realm of time and enter the spiritual world of eternity in which there is no time. The benefit of that spiritual world is that we do not have to wait to see the outcome of our suffering, but may know the end result at the beginning. The biblical promises of positive outcomes to all forms of suffering then become a great source of hope. It is this hope that allows us to persevere no matter how severe the trial.

The final point concerns the fact that they cannot possibly lose. All suffering implies that we have somehow failed and will ultimately lose. This sense of losing robs us of our personal worth during hard times. Again the Bible makes it abundantly clear that no matter what we must suffer, we will not finally lose. Although there may be many times that it will look like we are losing, the fact is that we will always come out victorious. God's method of dealing with us remains the same...death and resurrection. While it may appear and feel like we are losing during the "death", the "resurrection" proves beyond any doubt that we are more than conquerors.

Summary

Comforting the "feebleminded" or hurting people is a vital part of our relational ministry to others. The reason they are referred to as "feebleminded" has to do with the fact that how we think, especially in times of suffering, determines how we feel. In order to help them feel better we have to address their underlying beliefs about themselves and all the negative self talk that makes them "feebleminded". A mind filled with the false assumptions about our worth is, indeed, feeble and will fill us with frustration and pain in this sin cursed world we live in.

The relational skill of comforting others not only requires the foundation of personal and communication skills, but also the experience of God's comfort for us. God continually comforts us so that we may be prepared to comfort others with that same comfort. Unless we ourselves receive the comfort of God in our tribulation, we cannot really comfort others when they suffer. In addition, as we enter into the pain and suffering of others we also need the comfort of God to sustain us in the ministry of comforting them. It is uncomfortable for us to be around those who are suffering, never mind seek to comfort them.

Our own personal understanding of the eternal view of suffering and faith in the comfort of God is what prepares us for comforting those who are suffering. When we are willing to be honest about our struggles and to believe the gospel in the midst of our own hurt and frustration, we are prepared to share with others how God can comfort them. As in the case of the relational skill of confrontation however, we must be led of the Spirit in this ministry as well. Only those who are led and empowered by the Comforter are capable of truly comforting the hurting.

Exercises

1. The relational skill of comforting the feebleminded is built on a personal history of receiving comfort in our own times of suffering. Describe a painful situation in which you were comforted of God.
2. How has the eternal view of suffering helped you cope with difficult times or situations in you own walk? Write down some "lessons learned" from your own experience in times of suffering.
3. Because actions often speak louder than words, list three ways you can comfort someone without saying anything.
4. Briefly describe why even the suffering that comes from making a mistake or as a consequence of the self centered flesh can be viewed as suffering for the sake of Jesus.
5. List seven biblical stories or verses that prove the believer's worth as a person despite the things he may have to suffer.

13. Support without Strings

Loving Without Expectations

In addition to warning the unruly and comforting the feebleminded we are called to support the weak in order to love others the way Christ loves us. Often we are tempted to get picky about whom to love. We might not mind comforting people who are hurting, or even confronting those who behave inappropriately; but supporting the weak may stretch us a little more than we like. That's because the weak are not simply weak physically or financially, but are weak in faith. These are those who have a hard time believing the gospel for themselves. They do not really believe they are worthy in God's eyes and are desperately seeking love and respect from others around them. Naturally, they are continually disappointed in their relationships with others and spend most of their time and energy either whining about their wounded condition or trying hard to prove their worth to themselves and others. This makes them obnoxious

> We are called to support the weak in order to love others the way Christ loves us.

The relational ministry of loving one another, however, includes even those we find obnoxious…the weak in the faith. The difficulty here is that the weak are not capable of loving us in return, even in the humanistic or romantic sense of the word. Because of their weakness they cannot even think about others (except to manipulate them in some way), much less love us. We can expect nothing from the weak in the faith and will be sorely disappointed if we count on them in any way. The skill of supporting the weak, then, is best

165

viewed as 100% give on our part without any expectation of them appreciating or returning our love. No strings attached!

This skill is especially needful for parents who desire to raise healthy children capable of coping with a dysfunctional world. All children are, by nature, self-centered and incapable of really loving others. This is why God makes them cute when they are little. As any parent of young children can attest, loving them is a one way street for many years. It's not until they mature that they are capable of returning that love to their parents. Before they develop their own relationship to God and learn to receive their personal worth from him, our children are "weak in the faith" and will act accordingly.

Relating to our family members and others in a healthy way often involves supporting them in times when they do not believe the truth about their own worth and are acting out in some manner. Like the two other relational skills; the goal is not simply to change their behavior, but to change their thinking. Supporting the weak means we must again focus attention on challenging false assumptions (faulty belief systems) and replacing them with the truth concerning their worth as a person.

At this point it may be useful to note the way in which these relational skills interface with each other. When inappropriate behavior is in focus, we must warn the unruly. When personal suffering is in focus we must comfort the hurting. When faulty belief systems are in focus, we must support the weak. Over time, all these skills will usually be applied to the same individual as we seek to relate God's love to them. Warning, comforting, and supporting all have to do with challenging false beliefs concerning personal worth, but the skill of supporting the weak is especially focused on developing and building up a new belief system of truth in the minds of those we serve.

Receiving the Weak

The first step in supporting the weak is to receive them without despising them for their weakness. This is a lot easier said than done since those who are weak are noted for condemning others. In Romans 14 Paul gives us some very practical advice concerning this ministry. *"Him that is weak in the faith receive ye, but not to doubtful disputations. For one believeth that he may eat all things: another, who is weak, eateth herbs. Let not him that eateth despise him that eateth not; and let not him which eateth not judge him that eateth: for God hath received him."* The admonition to receive the weak in the faith is immediately qualified by the statement, "but not to doubtful disputations" which is King James language for, "not arguing with them about their doubtful issues". Doubtful issues are simply those issues in our everyday lives that cause some doubt in our minds because there is no clear definition or directive in the Bible. These are the issues of life that we must depend on the personal leadership of the Spirit to resolve in our minds. The weak in the faith have usually resolved such issues by their own knowledge of good and evil and continually rationalize and justify their position. This makes them "testy" and easily provoked to arguments to prove they are right. To receive such "testy" people requires the supernatural love of God for both us and them.

Note also that that the weak have a tendency to judge others who do not agree with their conclusions about the doubtful issues. Using

> Romans 14
>
> *"Him that is weak in the faith receive ye, but not to doubtful disputations. For one believeth that he may eat all things: another, who is weak, eateth herbs. Let not him that eateth despise him that eateth not; and let not him which eateth not judge him that eateth: for God hath received him."*

the dietary example Paul tells us that the weak (who adhere strictly to dietary laws) only eats "herbs" (is a vegetarian); whereas the strong in the faith knows that he is at liberty to eat "all things" (including meat). The relational problem is not whether or not we eat, but our attitude and actions toward others who are not like us. He warns the one eating all things not to despise or hate the one who is a vegetarian. The reason for such an attitude of hatred is not simply because the weak one is a vegetarian, but because he is continually judging those who eat all things as somehow unspiritual, personally worthless, and deserving of condemnation.

Those who are weak in the faith do not realize that they are worthy as persons because of what God has done for them, but think they are worthy because of their own performance. In the example Paul gives, the weak is ignorant of all that God has done to make them secure in His love and significant in his plan and, therefore, is trusting in his own ability to interpret and keep God's dietary law to make himself worthy of God's love and acceptance. As a result the weak are generally very proud and quick to judge others as being worthless. Trusting in their own performance and abilities to gain the approval of God and man, they are also sometimes very opinionated, intolerant, and generally obnoxious. These are the self-righteous folks who try to look good at the expense of others and are always comparing themselves to others. To receive such people is very difficult especially if they happen to be personally related to us as family members, co-workers, or friends. It requires mountain-moving faith on our part to believe that we are worthy when criticized and judged by them. And it takes even stronger faith to seek to support those who are critical and judgmental of our lives.

Like the other relational skills, supporting the weak starts first inside ourselves by believing we are worthy no matter what the weak member may think or say. Receiving the weak means that we simply do not react to their dysfunctional thinking and behavior with that of our own. We must learn to separate their true identity from their performance in spite of the criticism they may direct our way. The important issue here is not what they think of us, but what they are thinking about themselves. Find a miserable person and you'll find a person who is weak in faith about their own identity. Basing their own worth as persons on a variety of false assumptions, the weak member is really miserable at heart. The more critical they are the more miserable they become. They are caught in the vicious cycle of condemning themselves and criticizing others. To receive those means that we accept the real person God has made them to be (i.e. loving and healthy) while rejecting their dysfunctional performance. Supporting them requires us to focus on building up their new identity as a person. Supporting the weak requires supernatural strength!

At this point it is critical that we avoid any arguments about the performance issues the weak are depending on for their worth. To argue with them about the correctness of their performance will miss the more important point of their true source of worth. For instance, an adolescent who is weak in the faith may criticize his parents for being "old fashion" because they expect him to come home at a decent hour of the night. To receive him his parents must not react to his criticism with their own false assumptions (I will be worthy if my child appreciates and obeys me). Further, they must avoid arguments about the time of a curfew in which they would naturally seek to prove their own point of view. Instead, the parents may affirm the worth of their child no matter what time he comes in, proving that personal security for both the child and the parents has nothing to do with performance.

Likewise, a personal friend may insist on performing some sort of religious ritual in order to secure God's blessings on his life. This may be something as simple as a prayer before a meal or as complicated as involvement in various church activities or programs. To receive him will be to do our best to maintain a relationship with him despite the fact that he may judge you for not participating in his rituals. Rather than argue about the rituals being right or wrong, we can affirm his worth and accept him as a person despite his rudeness toward us.

Does this mean that we can never challenge the weak child or weak friend's behavior? Not at all! The question here is not about challenging behavior or setting boundaries, but rather the time and manner in which we go about doing that very thing. The relational skill of supporting the weak requires us to keep our focus on his thinking rather than his behavior. Not only do we overlook his judgmental attitude and actions toward us, but we also ignore his efforts to make himself worthy by his own performance. It is far more important to help him change his thinking about himself than it is to prove that our own actions and rules are correct. If the thinking can be changed, the behavior will follow.

Spiritual Enlightenment

The goal of receiving the weak is to give them the time and space they need to become strong. As noted above, this will require a radical change in their thinking. This change is so radical the only one who can truly make the change is God. The divine intervention needed to change the thinking of those who are weak in the faith is referred to as "spiritual enlightenment". Before we can expect the weak to feel or act differently we need to allow them to think differently. Using the previous examples we may begin to see our goal as allowing God to change the child's thinking about himself and when he should come home at night; or to allow God to work in the friend's mind to change his attitude about himself and what he should do about prayer and church activities. The important issue here is not what the weak think of us, but rather what they think of themselves…their spiritual enlightenment.

Receiving the weak in the faith is really just accepting them where they are without any strings attached. Although it may be difficult due to their judgmental attitude and critical spirit toward you, it is necessary to show them you really do love them despite their feelings toward you. Your willingness to love and accept them as persons regardless of their attitude or behavior is the first step in earning the right to teach them to apply the gospel in their own lives. To engage them in an argument or debate about their doubtful issues will not demonstrate your love and acceptance for them, but will hinder you from being able to help them realize they are worthy as persons. It is the spiritual enlightenment that they need to become strong in their faith; and our willingness to receive the weak in the faith is what gives them the opportunity to experience that enlightenment.

Supporting the Weak

In addition to receiving the weak we are called upon to actually support them. This does not mean that we are to police them or fix them in some way, but that we are used by God to affirm them as being worthy. The parents in our previous example may set the curfew at 11 p.m. and be ready to meet out various forms of punishment if the curfew is violated. But that is not supporting the weak. That's "policing the weak". Supporting the weak would include affirming the fact that the child is worthy whether he gets to stay out as late as he wants to or has to come home at 11 p.m. The real question is, "Who sets the curfew...the parents, the child, or God? Supporting the weak in this case means that we do not fall into the trap of fighting over who is in control of the curfew, but affirm the child's worth and suggest that the curfew be set by God.

It may seem to be overly spiritual to depend on God to set a curfew for our adolescent child, but actually suggesting the idea starts the very process of change in their thinking we desire. Simply asking the child what they believe God thinks about their curfew opens up a tremendous opportunity to begin to challenge false assumptions and seek the spiritual enlightenment needed to make healthy decisions. All too often we find ourselves trapped in an argument concerning doubtful issues that can only be answered by

God. The appropriate time for a curfew is one such issue. There is no unalterable law of the universe that says a child must be home at 11 p.m. and the arguments pro and con are infinite. The only acceptable answer to such a question is what God says to both the parents and their child. This is called spiritual enlightenment. In order to truly support the weak we must learn to depend on God's ability to enlighten them personally.

"Let every man be fully persuaded in his own mind" is the answer Paul gives for all doubtful issues. In the verses that follow in Romans 14 he makes it clear that it's not a matter of who is right and who is wrong, but what the Spirit of God is leading us to do in any given situation. The amazing thing about God that most of the weak brethren do not understand is that he works differently with different people at different times. God may lead one person to eat meat and, at the same time, be leading another person to be a vegetarian. He may impress upon one person to observe certain rituals and tell someone else not to observe them. He is an infinite God of variety. No two snowflakes have the same structure and neither do any two people have the exact same finger prints. God delights in variety when it comes to his eternal plan for our lives as well.

Spiritual enlightenment simply means that we allow God to direct our lives through the personal leadership of His Spirit. None of us really knows what we should think, feel, do, or say at any given time. At best we may take an educated guess as to what is best for our families and us. But God knows exactly what is best, and the good news is that He is willing and able to tell us when we ask. The weak in the faith not only suffer because they are caught in a performance trap to make themselves worthy, but also because they really don't have a clue about hearing what God has to say to them and following his leadership. Because they cannot hear God they are left to their own natural means of deciding what is the best thing to do. They end up relying on their own understanding and interpretation of the Bible, their own feelings, or the opinion of others around them. Because we naturally learn how to live by "modeling" others, the weak in the faith base their own decisions on what they see others doing and think they are being "spiritual". Sadly, they are not "fully persuaded in their own minds" by the Spirit of God as to what they should say or do.

Lacking the personal skill of spiritual enlightenment, the weak are usually very fearful and anxious about their own lives. They are constantly worried about whether they have heard and are doing the will of God. This anxious preoccupation with their own spiritual condition causes them to be as selfish as those who really don't think or care about the will of God in their lives. The only difference is that the weak in the faith have a religious façade they must maintain in order to feel secure and significant. They become defensive and tend to overuse their natural defense mechanisms such as rationalization, justification, denial, and projection. One of the most common defenses is referred to as reaction formation in which they preach loud and hard against the very thing they are guilty of doing themselves. The net result is that they are miserable, tired, and given to self condemnation and criticism of others. In such a state they are incapable of fulfilling their true calling to love others. All they can think about is how they can make themselves look good as a Christian.

Supporting such folks will require helping them develop the personal skills discussed earlier. In order to become strong they must learn to change their thinking about their own worth as persons, manage their emotions, challenge their fleshly motivations, and follow the personal leadership of the Spirit in their lives. As we have seen, the development of these skills is not an overnight process, but rather takes time and a lot of practice through much trial and error. When it comes to supporting the weak there

> Supporting the weak as they grow up spiritually will be an ongoing process, not a spontaneous event.

are no "quick fixes". You cannot raise a child in a matter of hours, days, weeks, or months. It takes time for children to grow up into adulthood. Likewise, It will require a great deal of patience, longsuffering, and consistent love on our part. Paul concluded in Romans 15:1, "*We then that are strong ought to bear the infirmities of the weak, and not to please ourselves.*

Burden Bearing

Our primary role in supporting the weak in the faith may best described as bearing their infirmities or weaknesses. By infirmities we mean not only their inability to believe the gospel for themselves, but the resulting emotional, behavioral, and relational consequences. The weak are not easy to tolerate much less support because they are usually religious and obnoxious. Their infirmities are not only detrimental to themselves personally, but also present a host of relational difficulties as well. In addition, any association we may have with them will reflect negatively on us too. Jesus was constantly criticized for "eating and drinking with publicans and sinners". The religious people condemned him as the friend of publicans and sinners because he was willing to associate with them. Likewise he was willing to interact with the religious leaders despite their efforts to discredit him and plans to murder him. His entire ministry on this earth may be described as bearing the burdens of others.

In Galatians 6:2 Paul tells us, "*Bear ye one another's burdens, and so fulfill the law of Christ.*" Our willingness to associate with, tolerate, and identify ourselves with the weak in the faith is all part of bearing their burdens. In so doing Paul says we are "fulfilling the law of Christ". By this he means that our ministry to the weak is really a

> Galatians 6:2
>
> "*Bear ye one another's burdens, and so fulfill the law of Christ.*"

fulfillment of Jesus' new command to love others as he does. While our efforts to minister the love of Christ to the weak in the faith may seem to be futile at times, we may be sure that we will be as successful as was Jesus. Although it looked like he was losing the battle when they nailed him to the cross and mocked him, the resurrection proved once and for all that he was victorious.

Practically speaking, supporting the weak by bearing their burdens is what earns us the right to share the gospel of grace with them. The reason they are weak is because they cannot believe the gospel for themselves. Deep down in their heart they do not believe they are worthy. They don't see themselves as secure in God's love or significant in his eternal plan for their lives. Supporting them means looking beyond their religious, stinking flesh to see with the eyes of Jesus a frightened little child of God who needs to be loved and respected. We are going to love them unconditionally, accept them without demands, and forgive them of their failures. We are going to respect them as one who is important, honor them as one who has real meaning and purpose in life, and encourage them as one who is capable in Christ of fulfilling that purpose.

When our support for the weak is genuine and empowered by the Spirit of God it is not uncommon for them to drop the facades and all the game playing, at least in our presence. As a matter of fact, the weak will actually begin to seek you out and turn to you for the affirmation they so desperately crave. While it is tempting to set your self up as their "god" and begin telling them what to do, care must be taken to point them to their real Father in heaven to meet their needs. While your ministry to them will make them feel worthy, only their relationship to God can make them worthy. You can be used of God to tell them the truth about their worth as persons, but only God can make it real to them.

What they need more than anything else is to actually hear God tell them personally that they are his beloved child in whom he is well pleased. Once they have been assured of their identity from

God, they can then begin to ask him what he wants them to do and say in their everyday lives. The overall goal of supporting the weak is to give them the opportunity to develop their own personal relationship with God. Only the one who shed his blood for them has the right to tell them what to do about any issue.

Summary

Our ministry of loving others like Christ could not be complete without supporting those who are weak in the faith. To some extent we will always be called upon to care for "baby" Christians who are struggling to believe the gospel for themselves and apply it in their everyday lives. Assuming that we are indeed the full grown adult children of God, it is our responsibility as those who are mature and strong in the faith to support others who are weak. Although it is often difficult for the reasons we have described, it is nonetheless extremely rewarding. John bore witness to this fact when he stated that he had no greater joy than to know his "children" were walking in truth.

Like the other relational skills we have discussed, supporting the weak in the faith requires us to exercise our own personal and communication skills. Not only will we need to affirm our own worth, manage our own emotions, and question our own motivation; but we will also need the spiritual enlightenment to communicate the love of Christ to those who are likely to be negative, critical, and judgmental. Even though we may be tempted at first to withdraw from those we are called to support, our reluctance will invariably turn to real joy as we are used of God to love his kids, no matter what their condition may be. Loving others like Christ is its own reward.

Exercises

1. Being weak in the faith can manifest itself in two basic forms...religious and non-religious. Give an example of each form by describing the actions of the people in each category.
2. To receive the weak in the faith implies that we are strong in the faith. List out the characteristics you think make you strong in the faith.
3. In loving others like Christ it is not unusual to warn them when they are unruly, comfort them when they hurt, and support them when they are weak. Give an example of a relationship in which all three skills would be needed.
4. Although there is a great deal of overlap between receiving and supporting the weak, describe the difference between the two aspects of this ministry.

14. Conclusion

The highest form of liberty known to man is the personal freedom from our natural self-centeredness to love others the way Christ loves them. Although it is often described biblically in terms of obedience to specific commands, loving others with the very love of God is really a privilege as opposed to a duty or obligation. To be chosen and used of God to love others like he does is an honor that assures us that we are, in fact, truly significant as persons. In many respects, this calling of God is the most rewarding and satisfying experience a human being can ever know.

As we have seen, loving others cannot be done on our own. We cannot simply decide that we will love others like Christ and begin doing so at will. As a matter of fact, the example of Paul's conflict recorded in Romans 7 makes it clear that our knowledge of the law (command to love others) and will power (choosing to do so) is not sufficient to get the job done. The new person God has made us to be in Christ is still living in the same old physical body that also contains the flesh. As a result, we may want to love others, choose to love them, and even try our best to love like Christ; but we will fail to love on our own. This is why we must have what we have termed "relational empowerment". We all need the supernatural power of the indwelling Holy Spirit to actually set us free from our own flesh with its carnal mind and empower the new person God has made us to be to relate to others like Christ. In other words, we must receive God's love before we can share it with others.

The privilege of loving others may be illustrated by using financial terms. Suppose you wanted to help 10 people who were struggling financially. In order to meet their needs you wanted to give them each $1000.00. Unless you had $10,000.00 in your bank account you would not be able to meet their needs. But what if you did have that amount of money? Would you give them each a check? I doubt it. If I had $10,000.00 in the bank, I would probably not spend it all on helping the 10 people either. Why not? If I gave all my money away to them, then I would need someone to help me! So what would it really take to be able to give 10 people $1,000.00 each? A lot more than 10 grand! I would have to have more like a million in the bank before I would consider giving 10 grand away. Even then, I would most likely want to be assured that the money I gave away would be replaced in some way.

Being called to love others means that God is going to have to prepare us to do so. He is going to have to satisfy our needs to such an extent that we are able to meet the needs of others. Much of what we have discussed as the development of personal skills is simply the personal preparation needed for us to love others. As we develop the personal skills of cognitive restructuring, emotional management, behavioral redirection, and spiritual enlightenment we are really learning to live in God's love for us. Every day our soul (person) hungers for love and thirsts for respect in order to satisfy our needs for worth. The personal skills are simply the result of learning to let God make us worthy by receiving in faith all he has made us to be in Christ. As our needs for worth are satisfied we are prepared to truly love others in the same way we have been loved. Such preparation is what we refer to a relational empowerment. Through satisfying our needs for love and respect, God prepares us to love and respect others.

The Role of Faith

When it comes to loving others like Christ our responsibility may be summarized by one word...faith.

When it comes to loving others like Christ our responsibility may be summarized by one word...faith. Our discussion of the personal, communication and relational skills demonstrates the absolute necessity of faith in every area. With regards

180

to the personal skills, we are called on to believe the truth about all God says he has done to make us worthy regardless of our own performance, the opinion of others, and our circumstances in life. Concerning our communication skills we must believe that God not only exists, but that he is also continually leading us by his Spirit. In the exercise of our relational skills (actually loving others) we also believe that we have and are doing and saying what is needed to confront, comfort, and support others. As Paul put it in Romans, "The just shall keep on living by faith".

The personal expression of faith on our part is what establishes that vertical relationship between us and God. By depending on all that he is and all that he has done for us in Christ we can enjoy a real sense of personal security. Most believers can attest to the fact that their faith offers a genuine sense of love, acceptance, and forgiveness (personal security) that is usually experienced at the point of conversion. For the first time in their life they experience a real sense of personal worth and "the joy of salvation". Likewise, the Father wants nothing more from his children than their faith in his provisions. Our willingness to trust only him and his provisions for our every need is the highest form of worship we can offer. The expression of our faith in the development of our personal, communication, and relational skills not only empowers us personally, but also pleases the Father immensely.

In his summary of the lifestyle of grace, the apostle Paul singles out faith as the foundational factor in our ability to love others. In Galatians 5:5,6 he writes, *"For we through the Spirit wait for the hope of righteousness by faith. For in Jesus Christ neither circumcision availeth anything, nor uncircumcision, but faith which worketh by love."* Here the importance of faith

> **Galatians 5:5-6**
> For we through the Spirit wait for the hope of righteousness by faith. For in Jesus Christ neither circumcision availeth anything, nor uncircumcision, but faith which worketh by love.

above any religious ritual (circumcision) is emphasized so that we understand that our Christian life cannot possibly be determined by our own choices and effort. In contrast to religious rituals Paul reveals that the "hope of righteousness" (being worthy of God's love) is gained by faith in the supernatural working of the Holy Spirit. Waiting by faith for the hope of righteousness simply means that we continue to believe in what God has done to make us righteous in Christ. Doing so does not lead to apathy as some would suggest, but rather frees us to actually love (worketh by love) others. Depending on God to make us worthy gives us the hope we need to be able to think about someone other than ourselves. Those who truly believe they have been made worthy as new creations of God and are, therefore dead to sin and alive unto God are free, indeed, to think about others.

> Here the importance of faith above any religious ritual (circumcision) is emphasized so that we understand that our Christian life cannot possibly be determined by our own choices and effort.

In addition to the foundational importance of faith allowing us to break free from the natural selfishness of the flesh, it is also the sustaining factor in our relational ministry. We not only believe, on a daily basis, that we are worthy, but we also must believe in the personal leadership of the Spirit in our daily lives. In addition to believing who you are, you also must believe what God is telling you to do each day. The Bible is a revelation of who God is and who he has made us to be, not a rule book to tell us what we need to do. Those who would love others need spontaneous, minute by minute direction as to what they are to say or do (the personal leadership of the indwelling Spirit) rather than a book of rules and commands. As discussed in the chapter on spiritual enlightenment, we need to exercise faith each day in the leadership and guidance of the indwelling Spirit to determine what we need to do to love others like Christ. The good news is that Jesus promised that very thing when he told his disciples in the upper room that he would send them the Comforter. Not only does he comfort us by our new identity in Christ, but he also comforts us by leading us step by step in our daily lives.

The Role of Hope

It is the personal exercise of faith that generates the hope needed to continue our relational ministry of loving others despite real difficulties and opposition. Hope is that "confident and joyful expectation of our future" that allows us to "keep on keeping on" in spite of trials and various obstacles. When it comes to exercising the relational skills needed to love others, hope is essential to sustain us in our ministry. People aren't always easy to love. As mentioned in our discussion on supporting the weak in the faith, sometimes they can be very obnoxious and critical. In times of relational strife the quality of hope is what allows us to persevere in our commitment to love them like Christ. Likewise, our relational ministry may be outright rejected by those we seek to help. Again, our hope that comes from believing sustains us during these times.

A classic example of relational endurance prompted by hope is that of Jesus' love for Judas. Nowhere is the unconditional love of Christ more evident than in the way he loved the one who betrayed him. The Gospel of John records Jesus' ministry to all his disciples during the last hours of his public ministry (John 13-17). There we are told, "Jesus knew that his hour was come that he should depart out of this world unto the Father" and he loved his disciples (including Judas) completely. Knowing that, "the Father had given all things into his hands, and that he came from God, and went to God" Jesus gave his disciples, including Judas, an object lesson on relational ministry. He laid aside his outer garments, wrapped himself in a towel like a common slave, and began to wash their feet. By this gesture, Jesus was illustrating his continual ministry to each of them to prepare them for their own relational ministry. The washing of the feet illustrates the way Jesus is willing to wash away the defilement of our flesh to prepare us to love others.

When he came to Judas, he stated that one of them would betray him and they all questioned who it might be. Looking up into the face of Judas he answered their worried concerns by saying, "I know whom I have chosen: but that the scripture might be fulfilled, He that eateth bread with me hath lifted up his heel against me. Now I tell you before it come, that, when it is come to pass, ye might believe that I am he." Despite the fact that Judas had already worked a deal with the religious leaders to sell Jesus out for thirty pieces of silver, Jesus told him that he was chosen to do this thing so that when he did he might believe on him. How could Jesus do that? How could he possible be concerned with the welfare of the one who was set on betraying him? Because Jesus believed the Father and knew that his hour had come to leave this world and go back to heaven, he knew he could not possibly lose. His faith in the Father's will gave him the hope he needed to endure not only the betrayal of a disciple, but the cross itself. His own hope enabled him to love the very one who was to betray him.

The rest of the story reveals the tender way that Jesus discretely dismissed Judas to do the thing for which he was chosen and prepare the others for their work ahead. After the crucifixion Judas did believe. He took back the money he had been given and was so grief stricken that he took his own life. Although there is room for debate on this issue, it seems more likely that Jesus was effective in ultimately winning Judas by his enduring love. Some may argue that Judas was lost because he hung himself. But more likely, Judas was saved, just as the repentant thief on the cross, by believing in Jesus at the last moment. Regardless of the ultimate outcome, the example of how Jesus persevered in loving Judas illustrates the power of hope in our relational ministry.

The manner in which Jesus related to his disciples and others, especially during the dark hours around his arrest and crucifixion, provide us with a divine model for the way we are to love others. He confronted their inappropriate behavior without condemning them, comforted them without enabling their dysfunction, and supported them without expecting them to care about him. Surely the stress he experienced during that time was enormous, and yet he continued to display the love of God. At his arrest he protected his disciples and during his mock trial he exercised restraint in the face of false accusations. Even while being crucified Jesus asked the Father to forgive the soldiers killing him. While hanging on the cross he received the repentant thief and made provisions for the care of his mother. His love was truly amazing! And now we have the privilege of loving others in the same manner!

It is my hope that what you have learned in this study will help you experience that amazing love for yourself and share it with others around you. My prayer for you is that recorded by Paul in his letter to the Ephesians:

> "For this cause I bow my knees unto the Father of our Lord Jesus Christ, Of whom the whole family in heaven and earth is named, That he would grant you, according to the riches of his glory, to be strengthened with might by his Spirit in the inner man; That Christ may dwell in your hearts by faith; that ye, being rooted and grounded in love, May be able to comprehend with all saints what is the breadth, and length, and depth, and height; And to know the love of Christ which passes knowledge, That ye might be filled with all the fullness of God."

About the Author

By drawing on his 35 years of pastoral counseling John C. Glenn has outlined the skills needed to develop and maintain healthy relationships in the home, on the job, or in the community. His Bachelor of Arts degree in Psychology and his Masters in Bible provide a unique background for applying his biblical model of counseling to some of the toughest relational issues in life. While serving as the ministry Training Director for two of the largest recovery programs in South Florida, Glenn wrote "The Alpha Series" emphasizing the need for biblical self-awareness and the believer's true identity in Christ for a lifestyle of recovery. Glenn is currently the Senior Pastor of Alpha Ministries' "Church in the Woods". He and his wife, Sandi, live on a ranch in South Florida.

About the Book

Loving others like Jesus is not automatic or natural, but it is vital to a satisfying home life, productive work environment, and a positive community. "The Power to Love" is a concise overview of the personal, communication, and relational skills needed to develop and maintain loving relationships. The personal skills include cognitive restructuring, emotional management, behavioral redirection, and spiritual enlightenment. The communication skills include understanding the miracle of communication, knowing what to talk about, and being able to speak the truth in love. The relational skills involve confrontation without condemnation, comforting without enabling, and supporting without hidden strings. Together these skills provide the relational empowerment needed to actually fulfill the new commandment of Jesus to love others the way he does. Those who experience "The Power to Love" described in these pages enjoy the personal benefits and genuine freedom of loving others regardless of their circumstances.

LaVergne, TN USA
15 December 2010
208771LV00003B/1/P